George William Ross

The Schools of England and Germany

George William Ross

The Schools of England and Germany

ISBN/EAN: 9783337532598

Printed in Europe, USA, Canada, Australia, Japan

Cover: Foto ©Paul-Georg Meister /pixelio.de

More available books at **www.hansebooks.com**

THE SCHOOLS

OF

ENGLAND AND GERMANY

BY

GEO. W. ROSS, LL.D.

MINISTER OF EDUCATION
FOR THE PROVINCE OF ONTARIO (CANADA.)

PRINTED FOR THE EDUCATION DEPARTMENT.

TORONTO:
PRINTED BY WARWICK BROS. & RUTTER, 68 & 70 FRONT ST. WEST.
1894.

PREFACE.

This sketch of the schools of England and Germany was prepared with two objects in view :—(1) To indicate the development of public opinion with regard to education, and the form which legislation assumed in solving the educational problems which pressed upon public attention ; and (2) to show what courses of study educators abroad deemed the most suitable for the different grades of schools, and what machinery was used in carrying on such courses by those responsible for the administration of educational affairs. This involved the consideration of the different grades of schools, the accommodation of pupils, the training and licensing of teachers, inspection, State aid to education, etc.

In preparing this sketch I have drawn very freely upon the reports of other writers. In many cases I have used the language of these writers without indicating in every case the quotations I have made, so as not to disturb the continuity of my narrative. Every reference to practical work, however, which a visitor could see for himself, whether the language is my own or not, I have verified by personal observation.

Official regulations are given *in extenso* in appendices for the benefit of those more immediately concerned in the administration of our school system.

GEO. W. ROSS,
Minister of Education.

EDUCATION DEPARTMENT,
    TORONTO, (ONTARIO),
        6th December, 1893.

BIBLIOGRAPHY.

Reports of the Education Department, England and Wales, 1888-9, 1889-90, 1890-1, 1892-3.

Reports of the United States Commissioner of Education, 1888-9, 1889-90.

German Elementary Education—C. C. Perry—1887.

Methods in the Schools of Germany—John T. Prince—1892.

Prussian Schools through American eyes—James Russell Parsons—1891.

Studies in Secondary Education—Edited by Arthur H. D. Acland, M.P., and H. Llewellyn Smith, M.A., with an introduction by James Bryce, M.P.—1892.

English Education (International Education Series)—by Isaac Sharpless, LL.D.—1892.

Magazines, Reviews, etc.

TABLE OF CONTENTS.

CHAPTER I.

Introduction.

Utility of reports on systems of education of other countries—Commission of 1836 under Dr. Duncomb—Dr. Ryerson appointed in 1844 to report on education—Quotations from his report—Report of 1868—Recommendations—Report on technical education by Dr. Hodgins in 1871—Further reports in 1885—Visit to Indian and Colonial Exhibition in 1886—Visit to England and the continent in 1892. Pages 9 to 22.

CHAPTER II.

The Elementary Schools of England and Wales.

Historical Sketch—The Monitorial system under Lancaster and Bell—Organization of the British and Foreign Society and the National Society for the promotion of education—Parliamentary intervention—Commissions of 1816, 1832, 1868—Mr. Forster's Act of 1870—Lord Sandon's Act—Compulsory attendance—Commission of 1886—Payment by results—Religious education—Relative standing of Board and Voluntary Schools—Results of twenty years' legislation—Education Act, 1891. Pages 23 to 41.

CHAPTER III.

Course of Study in Elementary Schools.

Course of study—Compulsory subjects—Optional or Class subjects—Specific subjects—Needlework for girls—Basis on which Government grant is paid—Comparison with Ontario—Night or Continuation schools. Pages 43 to 53.

CHAPTER IV.

Training of Teachers.

History of Training Colleges—Course of study—Cost of training—Comparison with Ontario—Opinions of Dr. Fitch—English system contrasted with Ontario. Pages 45 to 69.

CHAPTER V.

Inspection.

Inspectors, how appointed—Qualifications of—Number on staff—Instructions of Education Department—Value of such instructions to Ontario—Cost of Inspection—General remarks. Pages 71 to 84.

CHAPTER VI.

Secondary Schools.

Historical sketch—Classes of Secondary Schools—Public Schools—Courses of study—Westminster—Winchester—Eton—Rugby—Games and sports—Value of discipline—Grammar schools—Proprietary schools—Charity schools—Lord Taunton's report—Endowed Schools—Professor Bryce on training of teachers in Secondary Schools—Value of Secondary education. Pages 85 to 107.

CHAPTER VII.

German Schools.

Historical sketch—Compulsory education—Statistics of attendance—Classification of schools—Elementary schools—Instruction in Science—Course of study—Religious instruction—Continuation schools—Private Schools. Pages 109 to 128.

CHAPTER VIII.

German Secondary Schools.

Sketch—Classes of schools—The Gymnasium—Time-table—Real Schools—Leaving Examinations—Examination of teachers—Probejahr—Appointments—Pensions—Educational Conference, 1890—The Emperor's Speech—Comparison with Ontario. Pages 129 to 141.

CHAPTER IX.

Normal Schools.

Number of Schools—Qualifications for admission—Course of study—Criticism lessons—Examinations—Practical tests—Normal Schools for women—Examination of teachers in High Schools. Pages 143 to 153.

CHAPTER X.

Miscellaneous.

Organization of schools—Inspection—Mode of appointing teachers—Pensions—School houses—School terms—Text Books—Teachers' conferences—Grants to education—General Review. Pages 155 to 164.

CHAPTER XI.

General Conclusions.

Central Administration—Minister of Education—Local Administration—Managers and Boards of Trustees—Elections—Grades of teachers—Training Schools—Inspection—Text Books—Place of Secondary Schools in English and German systems of Education. Pages 165 to 172.

APPENDIX A.

Courses of Study in English Elementary Schools. Pages 173 to 181.

APPENDIX B.

Courses of Study for Pupil Teachers. Pages 183 to 188.

APPENDIX C.

Courses of Study for male teachers in Training Colleges or Normal Schools, England. Pages 189 to 196.

APPENDIX D.

Syllabus of Course in Civics for Night Schools, England. Pages 197 to 206.

APPENDIX E.

Rules of the Education Department, England, with respect to schools, sites, buildings and equipment. Pages 207 to 220.

APPENDIX F.

Syllabus of Course of Study in Elementary Schools, Prussia. Pages 221 to 233.

APPENDIX G.

Syllabus of course of Study in Normal Schools, Prussia. Pages 235 to 243.

CHAPTER I.

INTRODUCTION.

Commissions Appointed to Report on Systems of Education by other Countries—Commission of 1836 under Dr. Duncombe — Dr. Ryerson appointed to Report on Education in 1844—Quotations from his Report—Report of 1868—Recommendations—Report on Technical Education by Dr. Hodgins in 1871— Further Reports in 1885—Visit to India and Colonial Exhibition in 1886 — Visit to England and the Continent in 1892.

The practice of all enlightened countries in dealing with the great educational problems which force themselves upon public attention has been to consider the experience of other countries under similar circumstances, and by a careful study of the legislation which embodied their methods of dealing with those difficulties find a solution for their own.

As far back as 1837 Dr. Bache was commissioned by the trustees of Girard College, Philadelphia, to visit the schools of Germany, Great Britain, France, Holland and Switzerland in order to mature and perfect the administration of Girard College. Horace Mann and Dr. Henry

Barnard reported upon the Normal schools of the Continent before the authorities of the New England States undertook the organization of Normal Schools for themselves. The report by M. Cousin to the French Government on the Prussian system of education marked one of the greatest revolutions in the history of France which ever took place in that nation of many revolutions. The report made by Bishop Fraser on the school systems of Canada and the United States is among the most valuable submitted to the British Parliament. There were Royal commissions also—one under the Duke of Newcastle about thirty years ago, and one under the chairmanship of Lord Cross in 1886, that collected an immense amount of information which is being used every day by journalists, educators and others in their discussions on elementary and secondary education.

Every effort towards the organization of the school system of Ontario was also preceded either by the report of a Committee of Parliament or by an extended investigation into the school systems of the neighboring states, or of the different political divisions of Europe.

Among the earliest reports presented to Parliament, the most valuable was that of 1836, the Committee in this instance being composed of C. Duncombe, T. D. Morrison and William Bruce. By agreement among themselves, Dr. Duncombe was authorized to visit the schools of the United States for the purpose of ascertaining how far the legislation in force there would be of service in devising a system of common schools for Upper Canada.

On the 24th of Feb'y., 1836, his report, along with a draft Bill was submitted to the Legislative Assembly. Some of the best features of this Bill appear in the School Act of 1841 (4 & 5 V. c. 18).

The next effort to obtain information by which the judgment of the House and the country might be directed in further developing the school system was made in 1844, under the administration of Lord Metcalfe, by the appointment of the Rev. Egerton Ryerson, a commissioner to investigate the school systems of the continent, with a view (quoting the words of his commission) "to devise such measures as may be necessary to provide proper school books, to establish the most efficient system of instruction, to elevate the character of both teachers and schools, and to encourage every plan and effort to educate and improve the youthful mind of the country."

Dr. Ryerson devoted upwards of a year to the duty thus imposed upon him, and extended his inquiries into the dominions of nearly twenty Governments, among them Prussia, Denmark, Sweden, Holland, Belgium, France, Switzerland, Austria and Great Britain.

In his report, dated Education Office West, Cobourg, March 27th, 1846, we have an excellent summary of the salient features of the different systems of education which he examined—a comparison of which with the present position of the systems in operation in the same countries will show the gigantic strides that even conservative countries, like those above named have made in the promotion of popular education.

As the result of his inquiries, Dr. Ryerson recommended:

(1) A system of graduated schools composed of Elementary, Model, Grammar Schools and Colleges. The Elementary schools were intended to correspond to what was then called the common schools of Upper Canada and the Primary schools of France and Prussia; the Model Schools were to be Industrial or Real or Trade schools like the Polytechnic schools of Vienna and Paris, though on a smaller scale, or like the Real or Trade schools of Prussia ; the Grammar schools were to occupy the position and fulfil the functions of the French Communal schools, or Royal Colleges and the Prussian Burgher Schools and Gymnasia—the whole superstructure to be crowned by a Provincial University or Universities.

" Under such an organization " Dr. Ryerson says " The ame principles and spirit would pervade the entire system, from the Primary schools up to the University ; the basis of education in the Elementary Schools would be the same for the whole community—at least so far as public or governmental provisions and regulations are concerned—not interfering with private schools or taking them into the account; but as soon as the pupils would advance to the limits of the instruction provided for all, then those whose parents or guardians could no longer dispense with their services, would enter life with a sound elementary education ; those whose parents might be able and disposed would proceed, some to the Real school to prepare for the business of a farmer, an architect, an engineer, a manufacturer or mechanic, and others to the Grammar School to prepare for the University, and the profession."

"In the carrying out and completion of such a system, the courses of instruction in each class of schools would be prescribed, as also the qualifications for admission into each of them, above the Primary schools; each school would occupy its appropriate place, and each teacher would have his appropriate work; and no man in one and the same school, and on one and the same day, would be found making the absurd and abortive attempt of teaching the a, b, c's, reading, spelling, writing, arithmetic, grammar, geography, (in all their gradations) together with Latin, Greek and mathematics."

2. His second recommendation was that proper provision should be made for the training of teachers. In justification of this recommendation the practice of Prussia, the United States and Great Britain was cited and various quotations given from leading educational authorities setting forth the advantages to be derived from the employment of well trained teachers.

3. The third recommendation was that the text books to be used in the common schools should be selected by some competent authority, and that trustees and teachers should be limited in their choice to the books so selected. The example of France, Prussia, England and Ireland was cited as precedents for such a course.

4. The fourth recommendation referred to the inspection of the schools. On this point Dr. Ryerson's remarks are, notwithstanding our improved system of inspection, still worthy of consideration:

"As proper rules and a judicious course of instruction prescribed for a school, would be of little use without a competent and diligent master to execute the one and impart the other; so the enactment of a Common School Law, however complete in its provisions, and the sanctioning of a course of instruction, however practical and comprehensive, will contribute little for the education of the people, without the parental, vigilant and energetic oversight of the Government. If it is the duty of the Government to legislate on the subject of public instruction it must be its duty to see its laws executed. To pass a law, and then abandon, or, what is equivalent, neglect the execution of it, is a solecism in Government. Yet this is the very absurdity which some Governments have long practised; and this is the primary cause why education has not advanced under such Governments. After having enacted a law or laws on the subject of schools, they have left them—as a cast-off orphan—to the neglect or the care, as it might happen, of individuals, or neighborhoods, or towns—among whom the law has remained a dead letter, or lingered a feeble existence, according as the principal persons in each locality might be disposed to act or not act, in a matter so vitally important to the entire interests and highest prosperity of the State."

"If Government exists for the prosperity of the public family, then everything relating to educational instruction demands its practical care as well as legislative interference. Yet not a few persons have spoken and written as if the Government had nothing to do in a department which more than any other involves the heart and strength and happiness of the people, not to say the existence of a free constitution and system of laws, than merely to pass a statute and make certain appropriations—leaving the application or misapplication of public moneys, and everything practical and essential in the administration of the law, to various localities, as so many isolated or independent democracies."

" Under such circumstances there can be no system of public instruction; there may be one law, but the systems, or rather practices, may be as various as the smallest municipal divisions. To be a State system of public instruction, there must be a State control as well as a State law."

"The conviction of the important truth and duty involved in these remarks has led to one of the most important improvements which have, during the present century, taken place in the science of Government, the appointment of officers as well as the enactment of laws for the education of the whole people. Hence there is not a State in Europe, from despotic Russia down to the smallest Canton of republican Switzerland, which has not its council, or board, or minister, or superintendent, or prefect of public instruction, exercising an active and provident oversight, co-extensive with the provisions of the law and the community concerned. The most advanced of the neighboring States have found it necessary to adopt this as well as other educational improvements of European civilization. And it is now generally admitted, that the education of the people is more dependent upon the administration than upon the provisions of the laws relating to public instruction."

5. As a fifth recommendation the importance of conferences of teachers, local superintendents and school trustees was duly emphasized, both for the purpose of exciting to emulation in the great work of education and as a means of educating the public mind into a clearer conception of the responsibilities of the State with respect to educational reforms. In the same connection it was recommended that circulating libraries be provided in order that the work of education begun in the Common School might be continued in the homes of the pupil.

In summing up his report he said:

"The completion of the structure of which I have endeavored to lay the foundation and furnish the plan, must be the work of years, perhaps of an age. It is, however, a ground of encouragement and confidence, that we are not left to rude conjectures or untried theories in this work. For the prosecution of every part of it, even to the child's First Book, the most trifling article of furniture, the minutest detail of school order and school teaching, we have the brightest light of learning and experience; and we cannot fail of the completest success, if every legislator, and ruler, and ecclesiastic, and inspector, and trustee, and parent in the land will cultivate the spirit and imitate the example of the Prussian School Counsellor, Dinter, who commenced forty years prodigious labors, self denials, and charities with the engagement: 'I promised God that I will look upon every Prussian peasant child as a being who could complain of me before God, if I do not provide him the best education, as a man and a Christian, which it was possible for me to provide.'"

As the result of this report, so practical with regard to details and so comprehensive in its outlines of the system of education which he believed necessary, the old Parliament of Canada passed the School Act of 1851, which is practically the foundation of the present school system of the Province of Ontario.

The Common Schools then established are the Public Schools of to-day broadened at their base by the Kindergarten system, as recognized by law in 1885. The Grammar Schools recommended in 1846 are the High Schools of to-day, expanded into Collegiate Institutes with a curriculum as comprehensive as the colleges and academies of France or the gymnasia of Germany. Local superintendents are represented by County Inspectors. Normal Schools for the training of teachers, then recommended, have been established and have expanded on the one hand into County Model Schools for the training of 3rd Class teachers, and, on the other hand, into the School of Pedagogy for the training of High School masters. The Model Schools recommended by Dr. Ryerson, though not established in the form indicated in his report, have nevertheless their counterpart in the Art Schools for the training of artisans, in the School of Practical Science for the education of mechanics, of engineers, and in the Agricultural College for the education of farmers. The teachers' conferences have developed into the Teachers' Institutes of to-day under the direction and supervision of the Education Department, and the circulating libraries are represented by nearly

300 libraries in connection with our Mechanics' Institutes and by the large free libraries in our leading towns and cities. The Provincial University, which at that time had no independent existence as a State institution, has developed into one of the most powerful universities of the continent of America.

In every department of education there have been expansion and development. Even the functions of the Government with respect to education, as outlined in 1846 have been practically followed.

" These were, as defined by Dr. Ryerson :

" (1) To see that the Legislative grants are faithfully and judiciously expended according to the intentions of the Legislature ; that the conditions on which the appropriation have been made are in all cases fulfilled.

" (2) To see that the general principles of the law, as well as the objects of its appropriations, are in no instance contravened.

" (3) To prepare the regulations which relate to the general character and management of the schools and the qualifications and characters of the teachers—leaving the employment of them to the people, and a large discretion as to modes of teaching.

" (4) To provide or recommend books, the catalogue of which may enable trustees or committees to select suitable ones for the use of their schools.

" (5) To prepare and recommend suitable plans of school houses and their furniture and appendages, as one of the most important subsidiary means of good schools.

"(6) To employ every constitutional means to excite a spirit of intellectual activity and inquiry, and to satisfy it as far as possible by aiding in the establishment and selection of libraries and other means of diffusing useful knowledge.

"(7) Finally and especially, to see that an efficient system of inspection is exercised over all the schools. This involves the examination and licensing of teachers, visiting the schools, discovering errors, and suggesting remedies as to the organization, classification and methods of teaching in the schools, giving counsel and instruction as to their management, carefully examining the pupils, animating teachers, trustees and parents, by conversations, addresses, etc., whenever practicable, imparting vigor by every available means to the whole system."

Subsequent visits were made by Dr. Ryerson in 1850-1, 1855-6, 1866-7 to the United States and Europe for the purpose of further improving the School system of the Province. The only substantial changes recommended, are contained in the report of 1867-8 and are briefly as follows:

(1) That inspections by means of local superintendents appointed by County Councils be abolished, and a system of inspection by County Inspectors of undoubted qualifications and experience be adopted.

(2) That County Boards of Examiners with recognized qualifications be substituted for the boards previously established under the Act of 1851.

(3) That first-class certificates be made permanent.

(4) That a fixed minimum salary be secured for every teacher; such minimum to be prescribed by the County Board, the County Council or the Legislative Assembly.

(5) That adequate accommodation be provided for every school, and a limit placed upon the alteration of school sections.

(6) That power be given for the establishment of County Boards.

(7) That a High School be provided for girls.

(8) That all Public Schools be made free schools.

(9) That elementary education be compulsory.

(10) That no teacher be dismissed by a Board of Trustees without the concurrence of the Inspector

Of the recommendations made in 1867-8 all were embodied by the Legislature in the School Act of 1871, with the exception of three—that relating to the minimum salary for teachers, the dismissal of teachers without the concurrence of the Inspector, and the establishment of a High School for girls.

Since 1868 no formal report has been submitted, either on American or Continental systems of education. In 1870 a Commission, composed of J. G. Hodgins, LL.D., Deputy Superintendent of Education, and A. T. Macnattie, M.D., was appointed to report on Schools of Technical Science in the United States. Their report, which was presented to the Legislature in 1871, was the basis of the organization of the School of Technology.

In 1886 I had the honor to report upon the same subject, particularly with reference to engineering and practical science. The information thus acquired led to the expansion of the School of Technology under its new name of the "School of Practical Science," and to the establishment of the departments of Metallurgy and Assaying, electrical and hydraulic engineering and a department for instruction in Architecture.

In 1886 I had the pleasure of visiting, on behalf of the Ontario Government, the Indian and Colonial Exhibition held in the city of London. The Province of Ontario was permitted to make an exhibit of the work of its Public Schools, Art Schools, and Mechanics' Institutes—an exhibit which was regarded as creditable to the Province and which secured for us the distinction of many medals and certificates of honor. In connection with that visit I obtained from the Education Department of the United Kingdom of Great Britain and Ireland, and through the courtesy of Her Majesty's officers, a great deal of information with regard to the systems of education prevailing in the United Kingdom and in the different Colonies of the Empire. I also made a personal examination of the elementary schools in different parts of the kingdom and observed for myself their organization, discipline, course of study, etc. I visited several training schools or, as we would call them, Normal Schools, to see how far the methods adopted for the training of teachers could, with profit, be applied to our own Provincial Normal and Model Schools.

Again in 1892 I repeated my visit, going over much of the same ground, but with better opportunity for examining into details. Being favored with an extended leave of absence, I also visited France and Germany, and although at some disadvantage from an inadequate knowledge of the French and German languages, I was nevertheless able to understand from personal inspection and from contact with French and German educators, the distinguishing features of their respective systems.

In the report which follows I have attempted to give such sketches of an historical and legislative character as may, I trust, be found helpful in forming a broader opinion with respect to the great problems of education which confront educational reformers on both sides of the Atlantic.

CHAPTER II.

THE ELEMENTARY SCHOOLS OF ENGLAND AND WALES.

Historical Sketch—The Monitorial System under Lancaster and Bell—Organization of the British and Foreign Society—The National Society for the Promotion of Education—Parliamentary Intervention—Commissions of 1816, 1832, 1868—Mr. Forster's Act of 1870—Lord Sandon's Act—Compulsory Attendance —Commission of 1886—Payment by Results—Religious Education—Relative Standing of Board and Voluntary Schools—Results of 20 years' Legislation— Education Act, 1891.

No one who visits the office of the Education Department at Whitehall with its scores of clerks and large staff of inspectors and assistant inspectors would ever suppose that the system of education as now directed by " My Lords of the Privy Council" was hardly a quarter of a century old. Yet such is really the case. Although liberal provision had been made for the education of the middle and wealthier classes by the establishment of endowed schools, of which there are about 4,000 still in existence, the education of the masses prior to 1870 was entirely dependent upon the voluntary contributions of the people themselves. Many of these schools were kept in the most wretched hovels and were taught by persons of very inferior qualifications. The first educational movement which attracted general attention was that inaugurated by Joseph Lancaster in 1798, who opened a school for the artizan classes of London, and gathered around him nearly 1,000 children. Having no adult assistants or money to pay them he organized a corps of the older boys to take charge of the rest, and instruct them under his supervision. The school was divided into classes under monitors and superintending monitors, and was said to be a striking spectacle of order and mental activity. Mr. Lancaster's school, as would be expected, he being a non-conformist, was entirely non-sectarian, and as a rule was mainly supported by dissenters.

About the same time Dr. Andrew Bell opened a school which was conducted on the Monitorial system also. Dr. Bell belonged to the Church of England, and as the church catechism and liturgy formed a substantial part of the education given in his schools, he received the support of bishops, clergy and churchmen generally.

On account of the attitude of these two educational leaders to the established church, the people ranged themselves around each leader according as they were dissenters or supporters of the established church. The Lancasterians afterwards became known as the "British and Foreign School Society," and the disciples of Dr. Bell as the "National Society" for the education of the poor in the principles of the established church.

Under these two societies, schools were established in all the great towns of England. Fees were charged varying with the industrial and social condition of the places in which the schools were situated, and various reforms in the courses of study suited to the wants of the public were introduced. They were, however, purely voluntary. They received at first no State aid. The majority of the teachers were boys or girls of 14 or 15 years of age, in some cases younger. They were weak in organization and necessarily weak in discipline, but they were the harbingers of an educational development the most remarkable of the century.

Parliamentary Intervention.—Practically it may be said that the first sign of interest in public instruction evinced by Parliament was the appointment in 1816 of a select committee of the House of Commons on the education of the lower classes of the Metropolis. It was presided over by Mr. Henry Brougham, and reported the following year that " there was reason to conclude that a very large number of poor children were wholly without the means of instruction, although their parents appeared to be very desirous of obtaining that advantage for them. The committee enforced strongly the necessity for some measures whereby the deficiency in the means of instruction might be supplied, but no immediate action was taken on this report.

In 1832 Lord Althorp procured the assent of the House of Commons to a vote of £20,000 for the erection of school buildings in England. This sum was distributed through the Treasury Department to the National Society and the British and Foreign School Society. The grant did not apply to the maintenance of the school nor the instruction or inspection of the pupils.

In 1835 Lord Brougham brought before the House of Lords a series of resolutions declaring that it was incumbent upon Parliament further to encourage the establishment of schools and to provide seminaries for the training of teachers.

In 1838 a committee of the House of Commons reported strongly to the same effect, and in 1839, by the establishment of a committee of council on education at the instance of the Marquis of Lansdowne and Lord John Russell, the first step was taken towards the foundation of the present system of public elementary education. The committee of council was to be composed of the Lord President of the Council and four of Her Majesty's Ministers, and to this Board was intrusted the application of any sums which might be voted by Parliament for the purpose of education in England and Wales.

By an Act of Parliament passed in 1856, the office of Vice-President of the Privy Council on Education was established and provision made for dispensing the grant hitherto distributed by a Departmental Committee, by a Minister responsible to the House of Commons.

Royal Commission.—The grant of £20,000 which Parliament had given in 1832 to aid in the erection of school buildings had in 1858 increased to £663,435, and the misgivings entertained by many persons as to the value of the results attained by the nation in return for this outlay led to the appointment of a Royal Commission under the Presidency of the Duke of Newcastle, who afterwards visited Canada with the Prince of Wales in 1860. In connection with the investigation of this commission, assistant commissioners were appointed to visit France, Switzerland, Germany, the United States and Canada. The report of the Rev. James Fraser, afterwards Bishop Fraser, the Transatlantic Commissioner, on the schools of Canada and the United States is one of the most valuable educational reports in the archives of the Education Department. In 1861 the Commissioners reported the general conclusions at which they arrived—the most important being that the existing system had already reached only one-eighth of the population and that the attendance of even this number was often irregular; that aided schools were far more efficient than the unaided and private schools, but that even in the best schools only a small proportion of the pupils, not exceeding one-fourth, were successfully educated, and that the system provided no check on the tendency of many teachers to neglect the rudimentary subjects and the younger classes. They recommended that one part of the grant paid to a school should be made by the Committee of Council out of funds annually provided by Parliament and that another part should be furnished by means of a county rate. They insisted on this with great distinctness. "The one way of securing the efficiency of a school was declared to be 'to institute a searching examination of every child in all the schools to which grants were to be paid, and to make the prospects and position of the teachers depend upon the results of the examination.'"

Regulations of the Department.—Following up the report of the Commissioners, Mr. Lowe, afterwards Lord Sherbrooke, Vice-President of the Council, issued regulations for the apportionment of the full Parliamentary grant in each case to the local managers of the school—the amount of such grant to be determined by the efficiency of the pupils as reported by Her Majesty's inspectors, in reading, writing and arithmetic, thus introducing in its most drastic form the system of "payment by results," a system which continued in force for thirty years notwithstanding the all but united opposition of the profession In 1867 there was a slight modification in the form of the regulations whereby additional grants were given on condition that the school staff should be increased and that one additional subject, grammar, history or geography should be taught.

The Education Act of 1870.—The Education Act of 1870 may be fitly called the Magna Charta of English education ; for great as were the immunities and privileges wrested by the barons from King John at Runnymede, they could hardly be said to be greater than were the immunities and privileges granted by the Act of 1870 to many thousands of children for whose education the provision hitherto was entirely inadequate. To W. E. Forster Vice-President of the Council, is the credit due for this

Act as well as for the Act of 1871, effecting the educational system of Scotland. The object of the Act was not to supersede the voluntary schools already established and controlled by the different religious bodies of England, but to provide, where the voluntary schools had not made adequate provision, a system of State Schools, or as they are called, Board Schools, for those for whom the voluntary system was insufficient. This system can be briefly summarised as follows :

(1) That either by voluntary effort, or failing that, by compulsory establishment of School Boards there should be a sufficient supply of Public Elementary Schools for every district in the kingdom. The basis of the calculation was that accommodation should be provided for one-sixth of the population.

(2) That every such Public Elementary School should be taught by a properly qualified teacher, should be open to the inspection of Her Majesty's inspectors, and should conform to regulations to be prescribed from time to time by the Education Department.

(3) That in all Public Elementary Schools, whatever religious instruction was given should be imparted at the beginning or end of the school meeting, and that an unbroken period of two hours in each meeting should be devoted to secular instruction.

(4) That a time-table setting forth in detail the hours to be devoted to religious and secular instruction should be publicly displayed in each school room, and that parents should have the right to withdraw their children from any religious instruction or observance of which they disapproved.

(5) That in schools provided or managed by school boards no catechism or religious formulary, distinctive of any particular denomination, should be taught, and no inspection of religious instruction required or allowed.

(6) That the understanding hitherto existing between the Department and the religious bodies with regard to inspection should cease, and that all inspection should be conducted by officers appointed by the Department.

(7) That the local managers of the schools have authority to pass by-laws for the compulsory attendance of children at school, where school boards were established.

The first weakness discovered in the Act of 1870, was in the clauses with respect to compulsory attendance. It was not enough that attendance on board schools should be compulsory so long as there was no law to enforce attendance at voluntary schools. The great mass of ignorance which Mr. Forster's Act was intended to remove could not be overcome, unless stronger measures were taken. Accordingly, in 1876, an Act known as Lord Sandon's Act was passed by which school attendance committees were authorized to enforce attendance at schools where school boards had not been established, upon all children from 8 to 14 years of age, unless they should have succeeded in passing certain examinations prescribed by the local authorities before attaining that age.

By the Act of 1880, under Mr. Mundella attendance at schools of local boards by attendance committees was made compulsory and authority given the Education Department to establish infant schools according to the principles of Kindergarten Education as laid down by Frœbel and Pestalozzi. The inspectoral system was also organized under the same Act. England was divided into inspectoral districts and a regular staff of sub-inspectors appointed under the direction of twelve chief inspectors. Arrangements were made for annual conferences of inspectors in each division, and for an annual conference of the chiefs with the heads of the Education Department in London, with a view to the attainment of greater uniformity in judgment and in practice in the work of inspection.

Commission of 1886.—In 1886 a Commission was appointed under the Presidency of Lord Cross for the purpose of making further inquiry into the working of the Education Act of 1870. Although the people of England had accepted the Board School System with unexpected cordiality, it was thought that portions of the country were still unsupplied with schools, and that many children of school age, notwithstanding the compulsory provision of Lord Sandon's Act, were neglecting the means of education provided for them. The extent and character of the accommodation was considered insufficient in some districts. There was also considerable discussion as to the amount of religious instruction which should be given under the State system. The profession was greatly agitated over the system of " payment by results," which was one of the distinguishing features of the Act of 1870. Under that system the Inspector in his annual examinations subjected individually, such pupils of the schools as were present, to a rigid examination both oral and written. Where a written examination was practicable, and in proportion to the number of " passes ' the Government Grant was paid. In some cases teachers were employed at a fixed salary on the understanding that whatever the school earned in the way of Government Grant should be paid them in addition. The profession complained:

(1) That to pay the Government Grant according to the number of " passes " was to ignore entirely the functions of a true education. The object of school discipline, they said, was not to impart a fixed quantum of knowledge but to arouse the thinking powers of the pupil, and so to strengthen and fortify his character as to fit him for the duties of citizenship.

(2) That an ordinary teacher might by routine and repetition prepare his pupils for the inspector's examination more successfully than the true teacher who, with a higher conception of his calling, devoted himself to the cultivation of the mind generally rather than the development of the memory.

(3) That payment by results led to cramming in its worst form.

(4) That no matter how efficient a teacher was, unless he "passed" a large class every year he would be unable to hold his position.

(5) That the system gave both parents and children a false conception of the purpose of an education.

(6) That it hampered the teacher in the adoption of methods which seemed to him best by the fear that they would not produce the desired results under inspection.

These were matters of great moment, and without full and sufficient information the Education Department or the House of Commons could proceed no further in the direction of legislation.

The report of the Commissioners, made in 1888, showed clearly the advantages of the compulsory legislation of previous years, both from the increased numbers in attendance at the schools as well as from the regularity of attendance. On the question of religious instruction, they laid down the following propositions:

"(1) It is of the highest importance that all children should receive religious and moral training.

"(2) The evidence does not warrant the conclusion, that such religious and moral training can be amply provided otherwise than through the medium of Elementary schools.

"(3) In schools of a denominational character, to which parents are compelled to send their children, the parents have a right to require an operative conscience clause, so that care be taken that children shall not suffer in any way in consequence of their taking advantage of the conscience clause.

"(4) Inasmuch as parents are compelled to send their children to school, it is just and desirable that, as far as possible, they should be enabled to send them to a school suitable to their religious convictions or preferences."

As regards the relative management of the board and voluntary schools, the Commission says: "If it be asked under which system of management that branch of administration which can be transacted outside the school is most vigorously conducted, it would be impossible to deny the superiority of the school board dispensing the money of the ratepayers. If, however, we look for the closest supervision of the school, and the most effective sympathy between managers and teachers, or between managers and scholars, we would feel, on the whole, bound to pronounce in favor of the efficiency of voluntary management."

On the question of payment by results there was a great variety of testimony. To abolish the system entirely, it was feared, would relieve the teacher from the responsibility which he ought to feel in the advancement of his pupils. The Commissioners evidently inclined to the view expressed by Mr. Lowe in the House of Commons: " I do not promise that the system would be economical or that it will prove efficient. But if it is not efficient it will be economical, and if it is not economical it will certainly be efficient." The Education Department, however, modified the system so far at least as to dispense with individual " passes " as the basis of the Government Grant, substituting the efficiency of the class for the efficiency of the pupil. By this change the Inspector now recommends the payment of the Government Grant on the basis of the efficiency of the school, and the teacher is relieved to a certain extent from the various restrictions by which for over twenty years he felt himself hampered. The remarks of the Commissioners on this point are: " After weighing all the evidence laid before us we are convinced that the distribution of the Parliament Grant cannot be wholly freed from its present dependence on the results of examination without the risk of increasing greater evils than those which it has sought to cure. Nor can we believe that Parliament will long continue to make so large an annual grant as that which now appears in the Education Estimates without in some way satisfying itself that the quality of the education given justifies the expenditure."

In this brief summary which I have just given of the legislation of the House of Commons with regard to English education, I have covered a period of sixty years, assuming that the grant of £20,000 made in 1833 was the first action of the British Parliament for the promotion of Elementary education. As a matter of fact, however, it may be said that the first substantial step taken to organize a system of Education in England was the Act of 1870 by which school boards were authorized to impose local rates for the maintenance of their schools. Up to this point the education of the people was purely voluntary. There was no recognition of the great principles so early recognized in Ontario, that every child has a right at the hands of the State to at least an education which fits him for the duties of citizenship. So far as individual effort is concerned a great deal had been done. In 1870 there had been established in England and Wales 9,563 schools attended by 1,152,389 pupils, with a staff of certificated teachers numbering 12,467, assistant teachers 1,262, and pupil teachers 14,304; the population of England and Wales being at that time 22,090,163. In 1892 there were 19,515 schools attended by 4,609,240 children, with certificated teachers numbering 48,772, assistant teachers 23,558, and pupil teachers 26,961, while the estimated population of England and Wales was 29,403,346. That a simple Act of Parliament could bring about such stupendous results in a short period of twenty-two years is certainly one of the marvels of the nineteenth century.

It is also to be observed that these changes were effected not by a subversion of the traditions of the nation or the overthrow of existing systems, but by supplementing them where their resources seemed inadequate. The voluntary schools which had been in existence for centuries were not interfered with except in one or two particulars :

(1) They were required to employ duly qualified teachers, and

(2) They were submitted to the same inspection as the Board schools.

Where these two conditions existed they were paid the same as Board schools. No preference was given to one denomination over another. That they shared in the general stimulus given to education is apparent from the fact that while in 1870 there were only 8,281 voluntary day schools with an average attendance of 1,152,389 pupils, there were in 1892, 14,684 voluntary schools with an average attendance of 2,300,377 pupils.

I have already said that these grants were distributed without respect to the denominational character of the schools. In 1891-2 the Government Grant to

Church of England schools amounted to .. £1,302,440
Wesleyan schools 115,617
Roman Catholic schools 171,975
Undenominational schools 228,396
Board schools...................... 1,419,377

or a total Government Grant in aid of elementary education of £3,437,806. Compare this sum with the pittance of £20,000 first voted by Parliament in 1833, and the extent to which the public mind in England and Wales has been quickened and the public purse drawn upon in the last half century for the support of elementary education, will be at once apparent.

Education Act, 1891.—But great as has been the progress of education under the Acts of Parliament which required the parents to contribute, in the way of fees, a portion of the cost of the education of their children, greater results still may be expected from the Free Education Act of 1891. One can hardly conceive that a Parliament which at first reluctantly gave but £20,000 for elementary education would within half a century thereafter practically assume the whole burden of the education of the people. There is not, in the history of educational progress anywhere, such a tribute of appreciation and it is doubtful whether any country can show such a marvellous diffusion of education among the masses as England and Wales during that period. To the great majority of those to whom the Elementary School is the only one available, this relief must be peculiarly agreeable. The old theory that education was a privilege and not a right has been set aside in the march of progress and parents who from their circumstances were unable to provide their children with the most meagre education have now been relieved of all anxiety in this respect. The effect upon the working classes and those whose social position was at best somewhat invidious and depressing is hard to estimate. One thing which may be fairly assumed is that the diffusion of intelligence will lead to the promotion of greater comfort and a higher morality and to the ultimate suppression of pauperism which so unhappily mars the record of the uneducated classes. The following memorandum issued by the Education Department in May last sets forth the privileges of parents, and how they may obtain free education for their children under this Act;—

1. "Every father and mother in England and Wales has a right to free education, without payment or charge of any kind, for his or her children between the ages of three and fifteen. The right to free education is not a concession to poverty, but is common to all classes alike, Any parent who has not got free education already may write to the Education Department and claim it, either alone or in combination with other parents.

2. The claim may be made in the following form of words:—" I (or we) desire free education for the child (or children) mentioned below, and I (or we) represent to the Department that there is at present insufficient free school accommodation in the district for such child (or children)."

3. The free education to which parents have a right must be unconditional; that is to say, must not be free while the child is in certain standards only, or be given on the ground of poverty, or be subject to any inquiry as to the means of the parent or the reasons the parent has for desiring it, or be free only on the condition that the child attends regularly, or have any other conditon attached to it. It must be wholly free, without any charge for books, slates, or anything else; and it must be at a school within a reasonable distance of the child's home.

4. When the Education Department receive a claim for free education on behalf of one or more children. they make inquiry as to what free school places are available for these children, and if the number of free places is insufficient, cause a sufficient number to be provided. In districts where there is a school board the school board is directed to provide them; in districts where there is no school board, if the free places required are not provided by voluntary schools, a school board is formed, and directed to provide them in like manner.

5. Parents who have claimed free education, but have not yet obtained it, must go on sending their children to school, even if this involves paying fees, until the free places have been provided in the way explained above.

6. The managers of all schools, whether they are free or not, are bound to provide a proper supply of books, slates, and other school apparatus, and cannot compel a

parent to provide books either by periodical payment or by purchase, nor can they refuse admission to a child whose parent refuses to provide them. But if a parent prefers to buy school books outright, so that they may remain the property of the child, there is nothing to prevent his buying them from the managers, or the managers selling them to him, as a purely voluntary arrangement and a matter of mutual convenience.

In their report to the House of Commons the Lords of the Committee of Council on Education (1892-3) say :— " We are glad to be able to report that the introduction of free education into our system of public elementary schools has been effected without much friction and no serious dislocation of existing organizations. The statistical returns also show an encouraging improvement in school attendance. We have reasons to believe not only that the number of children on the registers, especially of infants, has been largely increased by the abolition of school fees, but also, what is more important, that the percentage of attendance of older scholars and the numbers on the registers has materially risen."

" The inspection returns of August 31st., 1892, show that out of 19,515 schools inspected, 18,673 had accepted the fee grant, and the number of schools receiving fee grant had on 1st June, 1893, risen to 19,534. Only 142 schools have refused the grant.

Of the 19,515 schools inspected, 15,170 were free schools, having 3,429,577 free scholars on the registers. The total number of free scholars on the registers of all schools was 3,880,722, and the total number of fee-paying scholars was 1,126,257. The number of free schools and free scholars has considerably increased since the period covered by our returns, but we are unable to give the exact figures up to the present date.

One remarkable and encouraging fact in connection with the introduction of free education has been the increase in the number of school savings banks."

CHAPTER III.

COURSES OF STUDY IN ELEMENTARY SCHOOLS.

Courses of Study—Compulsory Subjects—Optional or Class Subjects—Specific Subjects—Needlework for Girls—Basis on which Government Grant is paid—Comparison with Ontario — Night or Continuation Schools.

Elementary Schools.—The pupils in English Elementary Schools are classified, not according to forms, as in Ontario, but according to standards. The standards range from one to seven inclusive. The obligatory subjects are limited to Reading, Writing, Arithmetic, with Needlework for girls in day schools and Drawing for boys in schools ranked above the infant schools. The optional or class subjects are Singing, Recitation, Drawing (in infant schools and classes), English or Welsh (in Wales) or French (in the Channel Islands), Geography, Elementary Science, and Needlework for girls. One of these subjects must be taken, in addition to the obligatory subjects above mentioned. The teacher is also allowed to give instruction in the following subjects, called Specific Subjects, viz., Algebra, Euclid, Mensuration, Mechanics, Chemistry, Physics, Animal Physiology. Botany, Principles of Agriculture, Latin, French, Domestic Economy (for girls), Welsh (for scholars in schools in Wales), German, Book-keeping, Shorthand, Navigation, Horticulture, Cookery (for girls), Laundry Work (for girls), Dairy Work (for girls).

From this curriculum, it will be seen what are the limitations of the English Elementary Schools. Every school, in order to obtain the grant, must teach the obligatory subjects, and at least one, but not more than two, of the optional subjects.

The examination in the obligatory and class subjects is by classes, not by individuals. Where candidates take specific subjects the examination is individual and the grant attached in proportion to the number passed. Of the class subjects, English and Geography seem to be the favored ones. Out of 20,940 departments examined, 18,175 took English and 13,435 took Geography. The extent to which Elementary Science is taught in the English Schools is very limited. The number of departments examined in this subject was 788. It is also somewhat remarkable that only 1,627 departments were willing to submit to an examination in History, and that only 90,070 pupils were presented for examination in all the specific subjects. From this, it is quite clear that the Elementary Schools of England follow strictly the course of study which their name indicates. At most, there can only be in any school six subjects of study, including Needlework, which is compulsory for girls, and

Drawing in the case of boys. The teachers are under no restriction whatever as to the text books they may use. Pupils are required, however, to have two sets of reading books for Standards I., II. and III., one of which should relate to English History for each standard above the II. The Inspector is at liberty to examine the school from any of the text books in use.

Government Grants.—The conditions on which Grants are paid in Elementary Schools are somewhat intricate. A few among the more general may be mentioned:

1. The school must not be conducted for private profit and must not be farmed out by the managers to the teacher.

2. The school must not be unnecessary.

3. The principal teacher must be certificated, or, at least, provisionally certificated.

4. The school must meet not less than 400 times in a year, which means that the minimum school year is at least 200 days.

5. The school must be visited and reported on by an inspector, except in case of an epidemic.

6. The Department must be satisfied that the school premises are healthy, properly constructed, lighted, warmed, cleaned, drained, and ventilated; supplied with suitable offices, ample in their accommodation for the scholars attending the school, and properly provided with furniture, books, maps and all other apparatus of elementary instruction. The internal area fixed by the

Department for each pupil is eight square feet of surface and 80 cubic feet of internal space, against twelve square feet per pupil, in Ontario, and 250 cubic feet of air space.

Children under seven years are considered as belonging to the infant school, and receive a fixed grant of 9s. per unit of average attendance, provided the scholars are taught as a separate department, under a certificated teacher of their own, or as a class, under a teacher not less than 18 years of age, approved by the Inspector. There is, in addition, a variable grant of 2s., 4s., or 6s. On the report and recommendation of the Inspector, a grant of one shilling for needlework and another shilling for music is given. The grant of another shilling if the scholars are satisfactorily taught to sing by note or sixpence if they are satisfactorily taught to sing by ear. In Welsh districts popular Welsh airs, sung to Welsh words, will be accepted by the Inspector.

The day schools for older scholars are paid the following grants:

(*a*) A grant of 12s. 6d. per unit of average attendance, or 14s. upon the report of the Inspector.

(*b*) A grant of 1s. or 1s. 6d. for discipline and organization.

(*c*) A grant of 1s. for needlework, to girls only.

(*d*) A grant of 1s. if the scholars are satisfactorily taught to sing by note, or 6d. if they are satisfactorily taught to sing by ear.

(*e*) A grant of 1s. or 2s., according to the examination in class subjects.

(*f*) A grant of 2s. or 3s. for each scholar who passes the examination in any specific subject, no scholar being allowed to take more than two specific subjects at one examination.

(*g*) A grant of 4s. is made on account of any girl who passes the examination in cookery.

(*h*) A grant of 2s. for laundry work.

(*i*) A grant of 4s. for teaching Dairy Work by a teacher holding a certificate, recognized by the Department as competent to teach this subject.

It must not be assumed that all these grants are earned in every school. The highest grant of 14s., to which a school was entitled on account of efficiency, had, in 1892, been paid to only 32 per cent. of the schools inspected. The highest grant for discipline and organization, of 1s. 6d., was paid to 71 per cent. of the schools inspected. The grant for singing was earned by every department, with the exception of 125, more than one-half earning the higher grant of 1s. for singing by note. Cookery was taught in 2,113 departments, 90,794 girls having earned the grant, at the rate of 4s. The grant of 2s. for laundry work was earned by 2,766 girls, in 141 departments. Military drill is taught to the boys in 1,352 day schools. Manual instruction was taught in 285 schools, science, in 513 and physical exercise in 1,703. School libraries have been established in 5,500 schools.

The amount earned by each pupil on the basis of average attendance in 1892 was 18s. 4d. 3 fars., or a total

Parliamentary grant for Elementary education of £3,561,300 2s. 6d. In this mode of paying the grant there may be something for the Legislature and people of Ontario worthy of consideration. As the grant in Ontario is paid on the basis of average attendance, the poorly-conducted school earns as much money as the well-conducted school, the only practical difference being that the well-equipped and well-conducted school may possibly draw a larger and more regular attendance of pupils. The Inspector has the right to recommend the withholding of the school grant where the school is inefficient, but this is seldom done, so that, as a matter of practice, the Government grant is not much of a stimulus either to pupils, teachers or trustees. In England the case is materially altered, the principal grant of 12s. 6d., which may be held back but which cannot be abated, may be increased to 14s. on the report of the Inspector as to efficiency ; and in the same way other grants may be earned to a considerable amount by the energy of the teachers, the managers and the pupils. The principles followed in England with regard to the Elementary schools, but with greater detail, and, I believe, with greater justice as to the basis upon which a school grant should be paid, applies to the grants payable to High Schools in Ontario. In their case there is a fixed grant which a school is supposed to earn if it gets any grant at all, and, in addition, there is a grant for a library, for physical and chemical apparatus, for maps and globes, for a gymnasium, for teachers' salaries and for average attendance.

These grants apply to a school in all its essential features, viz., the school premises, the equipment and the teaching staff. If some similar scheme could be devised for the payment of grants for Public Schools, I am satisfied the effect would be, as in the case of High Schools, most stimulating. When trustees and teachers are in a legitimate way, by the expenditure of a moderate amount of money, or by a special effort in the administration of a school, enabled to increase their revenues, they are, as a rule, most ready to make that effort. Should it be possible to increase the grant to the Public Schools so as to subdivide it, as the High School grant is divided, a similar scheme could without any difficulty be adopted; but this rests upon the liberality of the Legislature.

Night or Continuation Schools.—Besides the provision made for Elementary education, the night schools receive annual grants from Parliament, according to a schedule framed on the same principles as the grants are paid to the day schools. The number of Departments, or what is the same thing, the number of night schools established in 1892, was 1,604, with an average attendance of 65,561 pupils above twelve years of age. The grant paid was £36,610 4s. A portion of this sum was paid to 3,531 girls in 198 schools for successfully passing the examination in cookery.

The object of the night school is to enable boys and girls whose occupations during the day render it impossible for them to continue their studies in the day school, to continue their studies. The instruction is simply a continuation of the work of the day school, and embraces the elementary subjects of Reading, Writing, Arithmetic, English Subjects, Geography and History, the languages, Mathematics, Science and Vocal Music. For girls and women the additional subjects of Domestic Economy, Needlework, Cookery, Laundry and Dairy Work are allowed. Instruction may also be given in other secular subjects and in religious subjects, but no grant is made in respect to any such instruction. Physical exercises and military drill are recognized for boys and men as a proper course in connection with the subjects of study. Any person over eighteen years of age approved by the Inspector, and not being a pupil-teacher engaged in a Public Elementary School, may be recognized as teacher or assistant teacher. The teachers need not be lay persons, but the principal teacher must be certificated or hold an equivalent rank. The school must meet not less than thirty evenings in the school year. The grant is paid according to the number of hours during which the pupils receive instruction. The course in Science and Practical Utility is very comprehensive, and includes Elementary Physiography, Elementary Physics and Chemistry, Science of Common Things, Mechanics, Sound, Light and Heat, Magnetism and Electricity, Human Physiology, Botany, Agriculture, Horticulture, Navigation, Book-keeping and Shorthand. The course in Domestic Economy includes the study of foods and beverages—their properties, nutritious values, and functions, their preparation; clothing, the dwelling, rules of health, washing. In addition to these there has been added recently an optional scheme in Civics, the syllabus of which will be found in Appendix B.

A brief sketch of the growth of Elementary education in the City of London may be taken as an illustration of the progress of education in England during the last twenty years.

The Board Schools of London are managed by a board elected by the ratepayers for three years. It comprises 55 members, organized in ten or eleven standing committees. In 1890 the Board employed a permanent staff of 406 officers and clerks, at an annual expenditure for salaries of £59,990. Of this staff 33 members were inspectors and 6 were school visitors. There were also 275 additional visitors employed to canvass every district of the city, to search out children of school age (3 to 13) and to make a record of their names, the condition of their homes and status with reference to school attendance. The Board has charge of all Elementary schools. Voluntary schools, as in other parts of England, are under the charge of boards appointed by their own patrons. Under by-laws of the Board, all children from five to twelve years inclusive, are required to attend school unless they have passed the Sixth grade at an earlier age than twelve. The visitors employed by the Board succeeded in scheduling 786,350 children between the age of three and thirteen, of whom 615,762 were within the age embraced by the compulsory attendance by-law of the city. Ninety-one per cent of this number were enrolled on the school register. Of the 9 per cent. not enrolled, some were reported as being educated at home, or disabled, or unable to find school accommodation. The average attendance was 78 per cent. of the whole number enrolled. The increase since 1870 is as follows:—

                                                      Increase.

Number of children of school age..... 37 per cent.
Accommodation in efficient schools....159 "
Average enrollment ....194 "
Average attendance ....193 "

The total expenditure by the London board for the year ending September 29th, 1890, for maintenance was £1,758,868, of which 20 per cent. was derived from the Government grant and 72 per cent. from rates. The expenditure per capita for average enrollment was $13.74, and of average attendance $17.30. The teaching force employed by the London Board amounted to 8,712 teachers; of these 2,396 were men and 4,770 women. Of pupil-teachers there were 1,546, viz., 298 boys and 1,248 girls. The adult teaching force was equivalent to one teacher for every 62 pupils enrolled, or, taking the whole force, one teacher for every 50 pupils. The average salary for every adult teacher was $1,215 for head teachers and $415 for assistant teachers. Eighty-one per cent. of the teachers are classified as trained. Out of 438,056 pupils enrolled in 1890, 219,749 pupils earned the Government grant for proficiency in English; 122,492 earned the grant for proficiency in Geography; 2,224 for proficiency in Elementary Science; and 2,468 for proficiency in History. Besides this, 15,560 girls passed the examination in Cookery. There were also small classes in manual training and in laundry work.

Speaking of the effect of education upon public morals, the Chairman of the London School Board made the following remarks: "Notwithstanding the growth of the population since 1870, the number of juvenile offenders is only 3,872 in 1891, as against 9,998 in 1870. Of course, the establishment in 1866 of industrial and reformatory schools has had much to do with this result; and it may be that many juvenile offenders who are now subjected to the reforming influence of industrial schools would at the earlier period have been punished by prison discipline, and, perhaps, have inevitably fallen into the ranks of criminals. But when full weight has been given to these considerations, a considerable margin of good still remains, which may largely be attributed to the elevating influence of good public elementary schools. There are evidences on all sides that the average culture of the community has been distinctly raised. Good literature commands a more enlarged circle of readers, and the spread of public libraries, still more the inexpensive editions of standard works, are tokens of this wider taste."

CHAPTER IV.

TRAINING OF TEACHERS.

History of Training Colleges—Courses of Study—Cost of Training—Comparison with Ontario—Opinions of Dr. Fitch—English System contrasted with Ontario System.

We have already noticed the establishment of the Education Department in 1839. The first Secretary of the Department, Dr. J. Phillip Kay, afterwards Sir James Kay Shuttleworth, was evidently impressed with the importance of placing trained teachers at the head of every school under the control of the Department. The efficiency of the schools of Switzerland, Prussia and Holland, which he had carefully studied, he believed, was owing largely to the care which had been taken in the training of their teachers. The voluntary schools had not quite overlooked this important work, but much remained to be done. Dr. Kay recommended a grant of £10,000 in aid of the Training Schools already established on the voluntary principle at Westminster and Borrough Road. An attempt was made to establish at Battersea in 1842, a Government Training School, independent of denominational control. This school was, however, handed over to the National Society and the policy of establishing Training Schools independent of denominational agencies was abandoned. There are now in existence (1892) forty-three Training Colleges or Normal Schools—seventeen for men, twenty-five for women and one for both with a capacity to educate 3,200 students.

The system of training teachers in England is worthy of careful study. It usually begins at the age of fourteen when the pupils have finished the seven standards prescribed by law for Elementary Schools.

No pupil teacher can be admitted to probation without first presenting a certificate from a medical practitioner in the form prescribed by the Department and also a certificate from the managers of the school with respect to his health and physical capacity as a teacher. A certificate of good character is also requisite from the managers and master or mistress of the school previously attended by the pupil teacher.

"Scrofula, fits, asthma, deafness, great imperfections of the sight or voice, the loss of an eye from constitutional disease, or the loss of an arm or leg, or the permanent disability of either arm or leg, curvature of the spine, hereditary tendency to insanity, or any constitutional infirmity of a disabling nature, is a positive disqualification in candidates for the office of pupil teacher."

If these preliminary requirements are satisfactory they are then apprenticed for a term of four years and become "pupil teachers." During this time they are in the school room giving such assistance as they can. They are required to give twenty-five hours a week to school room duties. They receive a small stipend, and instruction to the minimum amount of five hours a week. They are examined yearly, and if they fail the period of their apprenticeship is extended.

At the age of eighteen a final examination is given to the pupil teachers and other applicants, the passing of which gives them the privilege of teaching as "assistant teachers." The succeseful candidates are known as "Queen's scholars" and are divided into classes according to their proficiency. They are then open to engagements in subordinate positions or they may enter a Training College or Normal School for a two years' course. The number of pupil teachers is limited to a certain percentage of the whole number of teachers employed. If they pass a "good" examination, conducted each year by the Inspector, the school to which they are attached is entitled to a grant of £2 the first year, £2 the second, £3 the third, and £5 the fourth year, and for each pupil teacher who passes a "fair" examination, the school may receive £1 the first year, £1 the second, £2 the third, and £4 the fourth year. The object in paying a grant on account of the services of the pupil teacher is to stimulate the Principal of the school in the discharge of his duties as instructor to such pupils, and possibly to stimulate the pupil teacher himself to stand well with the School Board and members of the staff.

Training Colleges.—The Training Colleges to which the pupil teachers pass after completing their probation are supported and managed by the voluntary societies. They receive from the Government a grant of about £40 a year for every Queen's scholar who passes the prescribed examination. Up to 1891 all the Training Colleges boarded their students, and thus for two years—the length of the training course—"students lived together as members of a family, no doubt stimulating each other by a generous rivalry, to stand well in the profession for which they were preparing themselves." In return for the grant made to the Training Colleges by the Government, the Education Department is allowed to prescribe a syllabus or course of study which the teachers in training are expected to follow. (See Appendix D.) The course for male and female candidates is identical except that female candidates may omit Algebra, Geometry, and Political Economy, substituting for these subjects domestic economy, sewing and cutting out. They are also limited to the study of one language, their almost universal choice being French.

During the first year, students are taught Reading, Penmanship, Vocal Music, either from staff notation or from Tonic sol-fa notation, English, including Parsing and Analysis, and Literature, Geography and History, Arithmetic, Algebra and Mensuration, the first three books of Euclid with simple deductions, with certain options extending to the languages and to the sciences. They are expected within the year to memorize at least 300 lines from the works of Milton, Byron, Wordsworth or Tennyson. A student who passes any of the subjects, except the first four mentioned, in his training course at a British University or at any other examination approved by the Department, will not be subjected to an examination at the Training College. The work of the second year is but an extension of the first year's course with a greater number of options and political economy added.

The literature for 1892-3 was Scott's "Old Mortality," Shakespeare's "As You Like It" and certain selections from Tennyson.

In the second year, teachers in training are expected to teach a class in the presence of Her Majesty's Inspector and to have studied certain parts of Herbert Spencer on "Education" and Quick's "Educational Reformers." In some cases candidates continue for a third year in the Training School where the course is still more advanced but along the lines of the preceding years.

The course in Science embraces Theoretical and Applied Mechanics, Elementary Physics, Sound, Light and Heat, Magnetism and Electricity, Inorganic Chemistry, Human Physiology, Botany, Physiography and principles of Agriculture. The examinations in these subjects as well as in drawing are conducted by the Department of Science and Art. Every student in Chemistry is required to take a laboratory course and to perform in the presence of the examiner the more important and characteristic experiments involved in the explanation of his examination paper.

The Training Colleges in operation in 1893 were as follows:—

Church of England Training Colleges	30
British and Foreign Society Training Colleges	6
Wesleyan Training Colleges	2
Roman Catholic Training Colleges	3
Undenominational Training Colleges	3
Officers in Colleges including Principals	363
Officers in Practising School "	56
Number of students in residence (Feb., 1893)	3,400

Government Grant....................	£129,557		
Students' fees.......................	24,194		
Expenditure on Teachers' salaries	54,101		
Total cost of training	176,495		

	£	s.	d.
Average cost per student for tuition in Masters' Training Colleges.........	23	7	9
Average cost Mistresses' Colleges	17	15	2
Average cost board, fuel and other expenses, Masters' Colleges.........	28	4	1
Average cost Mistresses' Colleges....	19	17	6
Average cost permanent charges, Masters' Colleges.................	9	3	11
Average cost Mistresses' Colleges	19	17	6

The annual cost per student in an English Training School including Masters' and Mistresses' Schools is £44 11s. 4d., or about $215.

A few comparisons with Ontario give the following results :—

	Ontario.	England.
Number of Normal Schools.	2	44
Population per Normal School	1,000,000	700,000
Number of teachers trained annually	428	1,648
Ratio to whole profession employed	5 per cent.	3½ per cent.
Fees of students	$ 5 00	$34 50
Average cost of tution...........	64 65	95 22

It is worthy of notice that within the last few years much attention has been paid, particularly in the Training

Colleges for Mistresses, to the application of Kindergarten methods. Every teacher in training is now required to take a course in Kindergarten work. On this point, Dr. Fitch, in his report for 1892, says :—" This special branch of instruction is not, and ought not to be restricted to those students who intend to take service in Infant Schools. I have always felt it my duty to discourage any very marked separation of such students from others. The future mistress of a girls' school will probably have the oversight of an infant class or department, and ought to be acquainted with the best methods of conducting it. She should, therefore, while under training, practice and give lessons in the infant school as well as in that for older children. Whatever is true and wise in the Fröbelian and Pestalozzian philosophy is applicable to all teachers and to children of all ages. The Kindergarten is an organic part of a complete scheme of juvenile instruction and is most valuable as a preliminary training of those faculties and aptitudes which have afterwards to be developed when the time for serious application arrives. Experience proves that the plan of examining all the teachers of the Training Schools in Kindergarten methods as well as in the methods of advanced pupils has had a useful effect in broadening the views of the different classes of students, and in enabling them to see their own particular department of school work in truer perspective."

As to the practical tests of a student's power to teach at his final examination, Dr. Fitch makes the following observations :

"Every student is required to prepare before my visit, full notes of three lessons, of which one must be on one of the three elementary subjects, one on either a class subject, or a manual or object lesson for infants, and the third on any subject in which the student happens to be specially interested. This list is sent to me and returned to the College the day before the inspection, with a mark showing the subject which I have selected. The notes of all three lessons are submitted, but only one is actually heard. No one can be more conscious than I am of the inadequacy of this exercise, or indeed, of any conceivable single exercise, as a test of so complex and multiform a quality as teaching power. Many of the moral attributes which go to make up the character of a successful teacher necessarily escape analysis, and cannot be accurately estimated by hearing a single lesson. But much can be measured—the fluency and accuracy of speech, the attractiveness of manner, the skill with which the class is handled, the orderly arrangement of facts, the effectiveness of the questioning and recapitulation, the command of illustration, and the final outcome of the lesson, considered as an effort to enlarge the range of the scholar's reflection or knowledge. In all these respects, the sort of discipline through which the student passes in our best Training Colleges, appears to me well adapted to its purpose, and to become more effective every year."

Modes of Instruction.—The mode of instruction in the Training Colleges still partakes largely of lectures by the teacher and the taking of notes by the students. It is but seldom that the teacher conducts either a viva voce examination of his pupils during the term or indulges in the seminary form of instruction which so largely prevails in Germany. As a consequence of this his standing at the final examination is determined largely on written papers and on the report of the Inspector upon what appears to be his teaching qualities. During his attendance at the training institute the teacher spends several hours daily for about three weeks each year in the Practice school either attached to the Training College or contiguous thereto. His work in the practice school is criticised, and its weaknesses and defects are pointed out and correct principles and methods indicated. The time spent in practice teaching is far shorter in the English training schools than the time spent in the Normal Schools of Ontario.

"When the student leaves the Training College after two years study, he is examined by an inspector, and, if successful, receives a certificate of the second class. This enables him to teach as a "certificated teacher." Those who have come up through the ranks of pupil-teacher and assistant teacher, without going to a Training College are also allowed to take this examination if over twenty-one years of age. After having taught for ten years a new examination, covering both theory and practice, may raise the certificate to one of first-class, Of the certificated teachers, those who have been "trained," that is, who have spent two years at a Training College, now number a little more than half the whole corps, and the proportion is yearly increasing."

For the sake of comparison, the course of training for teachers in the Province of Ontario might now be pointed out. The *first* difference worthy of notice is the absence of the pupil teacher system in this Province. Ten years ago inspectors were allowed to give "Monitor's." certificates to pupils with whose attainments he was satisfied, to act as assistant teachers, but so rapidly did the number of duly qualified teachers increase, that this privilege was abolished. No doubt the permission given a board of trustees to employ pupil teachers at the age of fourteen is economical and one from which, if the Principal of the school and his qualified assistants are men and women of capacity, reasonable results could be obtained. To employ pupil teachers, where a trained teacher is available would be to make the interests of education entirely subordinate to the complaints of the taxpayer. As a means of training teachers, however, a good deal could be said in its favor. Any person who spends four years in a school and who has to bear more or less the responsibility of management and discipline during that time, who receives regular instruction in methods of teaching from a capable Principal and who is familiarized with all the tactics of school administration cannot fail to have acquired much of what will afterwards prove useful professionally. Such a system notwithstanding all that has been, or can be said, in its favor has never found any support in the schools of Canada or the United States, and under present circumstances could not be made applicable to Ontario.

The *second* feature of the English training system is the combination of the professional with the non-professional course of training. This system still prevails in all the Normal Schools of Canada, excepting those of Ontario and Manitoba. The same system also prevails in the Normal Schools of the United States. The union of these courses of training is, however, inevitable under any system of education in which there is a distinct line of cleavage between the elementary and higher education of the pupil, and it was only in 1878 when the courses of study in the Public and High schools were differentiated and our High schools officered with men of University attainments, that the separation of the two courses was possible in Ontario. Many of the leading educators of the United States and some in England also, advocate the same policy for their respective countries and no doubt will make a change so soon as the conditions above mentioned prevail. I may say, however, that the combination of the two courses is not without its advantages. The student who is taught a subject from the standpoint of the teacher and with the knowledge that he will be required to teach the same subject himself by and by, necessarily gives more attention to the methods under which he receives the instruction than the student who has no other object in view than the acquisition of knowledge On the other hand it may be said that the student who has finished his academic course and who comes to a Normal school to receive instruction in methods is able to give his undivided attention to a consideration of the processes by which knowledge is acquired and retained and on that very account makes greater progress in the art of Methodology. No evil results, so far as I know, can be traced from the separation of the two courses in Ontario. On the contrary, I believe the teachers at our Normal Schools are as well trained as at any other Normal School where the two systems are combined, and at the same time our High schools and Collegiate Institutes have been stimulated into greater activity by the presence in their classes of young men and women preparing for the teaching profession.

The *third* feature of the English system of training is the residential character of the Training Colleges. Until recently all the Training Colleges like the majority of the English universities, provided lodgings for the students. In 1890 provision was made for attaching to the larger universities and colleges doing university work, day classes for instruction in the theory and practice of education. These classes were attended in 1892 by 146 males and 176 females. In 1893, lectures were delivered by the Principals of the Faculty of the University in the history of education and in Mental Science in its relation to the teacher's work. Some of the Public schools convenient to the College are used as Practice schools and are attended by a number of the Training College staff for the purpose of observing the work of the students and making the necessary observations with a view to future criticism. From the rapid growth of the day training schools it is quite evident, although they cannot supersede the residential schools they will very soon be an important factor in the training of teachers.

The *fourth* feature of the English training system is the length of the training term. This arises not so much from the extent of the course given in methods as from the necessity of prolonging the course with a view to the non-professional training of the students. From the syllabus of the professional course it would appear that the work covered is not as extensive as that prescribed in the schools of Ontario, and the limited practice, three weeks in each year, is certainly less advantageous to the student than the more extensive practice allowed in our Normal schools. The premium placed on experience by the Education Department of England, is worthy of notice. Although a teacher obtains his certificate at the end of his Normal school course, providing he passes the required examination, he is ranked simply as a "certificated teacher." If, after ten years experience, he submits himself to an examination in the Theory and Practice of education, and obtains the required standing, he is then regarded as a certificated teacher of the first class. This is the highest rank of merit in the profession.

Training of Secondary Teachers.—No provision has yet been made in England for the training of the teachers of the Public and Grammar schools. The College of Preceptors, an organized body of educators, holds examinations which are purely voluntary, but which nevertheless are accepted as evidence of superior pedagogical attainments. There is a small Training College in London for women and a somewhat similar college forming something of an annex to Cambridge University for women also, in which good work is done, and of whose courses many teachers avail themselves. The University of London holds examinations for those who have already received its degree, to whom it awards on passing the prescribed standard, a teacher's diploma. This examination covers the following subjects:

(1) Mental and Moral Science in their relation to the work of teaching.

(2) Methods of teaching and school management (theoretical).

(3) The history of education; the lives and work of eminent teachers: and the systems of instruction adopted in foreign countries.

(4) Practical skill in teaching.

The College of Preceptors also offers its diplomas to teachers who pass its examinations. These diplomas are of three grades, Diploma of Associate, Diploma of Licentiate and Diploma of Fellow, standing for examinations of progressive difficulty. For all, a certain amount of English language and literature, geography and arithmetic is required. There is also an examination on the theory and practice of teaching, embracing mental, moral and physiological science, school government, lesson giving, and criticism of methods history of education, etc., of increasing thoroughness for the different diplomas. The candidate for the associateship must also pass an examination on one of the following subjects, the candidate for the licentiateship on two, and the candidate for the fellowship on three, viz:

(1) Classics.

(2) Modern languages.

(3) Mathematics.

(4) Science.

These four subjects are supposed to be equivalent to each other. The mathematical requirements are:

(1) Associateship.—Arithmetic, four books of Euclid, Algebra, including Quadratics.

(2) Licentiateship.—Arithmetic and Algebra, plane and solid Geometry, plane Trigonometry and Logarithms conic sections, and co-ordinate geometry.

(3) Fellowship.—The above, and higher Algebra, with theory of equations, conic sections, spherical Trigonometry, differential and integral calculus.

One, two and five years experience in teaching respectively, are required for the different grades.

From the general development of education and the improved methods of training, the teacher's position is steadily rising in public favor, at least judging from the salaries received. In 1857 the average salary of certificated teachers in Public Elementary schools was £65; in 1877, £115; in 1893, £120 12s. 4d. The average salary received by certificated mistresses was in 1869, £58; and in 1892, £77 13s. 3d. Considering the cost of rent, service and clothing in England, these salaries are much better than the salaries paid teachers in the Province of Ontario. It is also to be observed that the number of female teachers is increasing in England as seems to be the case all over the world. In 1869 out of every 100 teachers of each class, 48 certificated teachers, 60 assistant teachers and 57 pupil teachers were females. In 1892 the numbers respectively were, 60 certificated, 79 assistants and 78 pupil teachers.

CHAPTER V.

INSPECTION.

Inspectors How Appointed—Qualifications of Members of Staff—Instructions of the Education Department —Value of such Instructions to Ontario—Cost of Inspection and General Remarks.

Prior to the Act of 1870, the National schools were inspected by persons appointed by the Managers of the school with the approval of the Archbishop of Canterbury, and the schools under the British and Foreign Society, by laymen appointed by the School Managers. When the Government undertook by the Act of 1870 to aid all schools according to their efficiency, it assumed the right to appoint its own inspectors. Many of those previously in office were however, continued, and as might naturally be expected were clergymen of the different denominations, under whose management the schools were organized.

Inspectors are now chosen, as a rule, from the Honor graduates of the great Universities, and are generally men of culture and ability. The teaching profession has complained that in the selection of officers to appraise the standard of a school, professional experience is not considered. In the Province of Ontario no matter what the educational attainments of a University graduate may be, he is not eligible for appointment as inspector, unless he has had five years' experience as a teacher, three of which must have been in a Public school. The value of experience has, however, been lately recognized by the Department under Mr. Acland, now Vice-President of the Committee of Council on Education. No clergyman can be appointed as inspector. It is the duty of the Inspector to examine a school in order to ascertain whether the conditions of the annual grants have been fulfilled and to report the results to the Department; he has no power himself to withhold the grant, but simply reports the facts and on this report the Department takes action. He may visit a school with or without notice.

For purposes of inspection, England and Wales are divided into ten divisions, each under the supervision of a chief inspector. Under these chiefs there are 104 inspectors, 50 sub-inspectors and 160 inspectors' assistants. Besides these there are two inspectors of Training Colleges, an Inspector of Music, a Directress of Needlework and an Inspectress of cookery and laundry work.

The instructions given by the Education Department to inspectors are very minute and are quite applicable to the corresponding officers in the Province of Ontario. A few quotations from the revised instructions of 1893 might be worthy of consideration.

Inspectors are advised to be deliberate in their work and considerate towards the pupils.—" All hurry or undue haste on the day of examination is incompatible with the proper discharge of your main duty—that of ascertaining, verifying, and reporting the facts on which the parliamentary grant is administered. An early attendance at the school is absolutely indispensable, not only on account of the greater length of time available for work, but in the interests of the children, who are far more capable of sustained exertion in the early part of the day. It is especially necessary to avoid the attempt to do two things at once, *e.g.*, giving out dictation or sums while hearing the reading of another class; retaining children in school in the dinner hour, and thereby not allowing sufficient time for the meal; prolonging the examination to a late hour in the afternoon; and embarrassing young scholars by want of clearness in dictation or in asking questions. As far as possible it should be arranged that during your visit of inspection no class shall be left unemployed. Infants should not be detained beyond the ordinary hour for dismissal; and other children whom it is proposed to examine later should be relieved by a short interval for recreation before that time."

Inspectors should pay due regard to sound principles of Education.—" Two leading principles should be regarded as a sound basis for the education of early childhood. (1) The recognition of the child's spontaneous activity, and the stimulation of this activity in certain well-defined directions by the teachers (2) The harmonious and complete development of the whole of a child's faculties. The teacher should pay especial regard to the love of movement, which can alone secure healthy physical conditions; to the observant use of the organs of sense, especially those of sight and touch; and to that eager desire of questioning which intelligent children exhibit. All these should be encouraged under due limitations, and should be developed simultaneously, so that each stage of development may be complete in itself."

The value of association.—" You should direct the attention of teachers to the chief consideration which underlies true methods of infant teaching, viz., the association of one lesson with another through some one leading idea or ideas. The reading lessons, occupations, and object lessons may all be usefully combined for one purpose, *e.g.*, if the teacher wishes to impress on her class some knowledge of a domestic animal, she may usefully combine the object lesson for general study of its structure; the reading lesson for a knowledge of its habits and character; some occupation, such as pricking the outline, to impress an exact knowledge of its form; a song or simple story bearing on its association with human life so that familiarity with animals, especially with domestic animals and a kind treatment of them may be fostered. On the other hand you should caution teachers against the mere repetition of the same exercises and lessons; the progressive character of the whole scheme of instruction should be constantly kept in view; and each exercise should lead up to something beyond itself."

Proper use of pictures and flowers.—" Pictures and flowers have been wisely introduced of late in greater abundance into infant schools and have added much to their cheerfulness and attractiveness. They should be frequently taken down into the class, and made the subject of conversation. It is not enough that the children should be taught to observe these things and to answer questions upon them. They should be encouraged in every way to give expression in their own words to what they know, what they want to know and what they think."

Kindergarten principles.—" It should not be forgotten that the principles which underlie the system of *kindergarten* occupations do not cease to be applicable when a scholar quits the infant school department. For example, elementary drawing, dialogues, picture and object lessons, the cutting out and inventing of paper patterns, modelling, weighing and measuring, and musical drill, are not only useful in diversifying the day's employments in the lower standards of the school for older children, but they will be found to increase the brightness and intelligence with which those children pursue the regular course of elementary instruction. Moreover, such exercises will serve as a valuable link connecting the work of the infant school with some of those forms of technical or manual training, which are now, with very great advantage, adopted in the upper classes of many good schools. It is one of the chief objects of the *kindergarten* to establish a right and harmonious relation between those lessons which are addressed to the memory and the understanding of a child, and those interesting manual and other exercises which call forth his active and observant powers. And this is an object which ought to be kept steadily in view throughout all the subsequent stages of a scholar's career in a public elementary school."

Modes of Examining Reading.—" In Standards I. and II. intelligent reading should satisfy you without much examination into the matter of the book. The mechanical difficulties of reading, which are to be found in the shorter words of irregular notation, should be mastered before the Third Standard is reached; but even in lower standards an attempt should be made to teach children to read in a natural tone and to break up sentences rather into phrases than into single words. As a general rule, but especially in the lower standards, the examiner should be careful rather to ask for the meaning of short sentences and phrases than to require explanations of separate words by definitions or synonyms.

A very useful practice has been adopted in some good schools as an aid to the intelligent use of the art of reading, and it may suggest to you an effective way of varying your methods of inspection. While one class is under examination, a higher class may be set occasionally to read in silence two or three pages of some part of a reading book with which they are less familiar, and at the end of a short interval your questions on the matter of the lesson may enable you to judge how far the scholars have acquired the habit of reading a book by themselves and mastering its contents. It is desirable that you should inquire what use is made of the school library, and to what extent the co-operation of the parents is invited in encouraging the practice of home reading. In some good schools the aid of the parents has been successfully enlisted, and they have been urged to hear their children read aloud from a newspaper or from a book for a few minutes at home every day. The amount of oral practice which any one child can obtain in a large class is obviously insufficient; and a little home exercise in reading aloud is often found to have an excellent effect."

Arithmetic.—" In Arithmetic you will continue the usual practice of setting, in all standards above the second, four sums, of which not more than one should be a problem, and of accepting as sufficient two correct answers. In the case of girls right methods and arrangement, and good figures, may excuse a slight error in one of the answers. But it will not be right to report that this subject has been *well* taught unless the greater part of the scholars examined, work the problem (*i..e*, not necessarily give a correct solution but make an intelligent attempt at its solution) and answer correctly three questions out of the four."

You should satisfy yourself that the reasons of arithmetical processes have been properly explained and understood This is a department of school work which has been much overlooked. There is in the elementary school course scarcely any more effective discipline in thinking than is to be obtained from an investigation of the principles which underlie the rules of arithmetic. It is therefore desirable that you should very frequently ask the teacher of the class to give a demonstrative lesson on this subject; and he should so work out an example on the blackboard as to make the reason for every step of the process intelligible and interesting to the scholars. When children obtain answers to sums and problems by mere mechanical, routine, without knowing why they use the rule, they cannot be said to be well instructed in arithmetic.

Mental Arithmetic.—Mental Arithmetic is a class exercise, and may often be satisfactorily tested by requiring the teacher of the class to give a few questions in your presence, and by adding at discretion some questions of your own. The object of this exercise is to encourage dexterity, quickness, and accuracy in dealing with figures, and to anticipate, by means of rapid and varied oral practice with small numbers, the longer problems which have afterwards to be worked out in writing. It is obvious that this general object cannot be attained if the exercises are confined to a few rules for computing " dozens" and " scores," such as are often supposed to be specially suited for mental calculation. Occasionally a long column of figures may be written in the sight of the scholars, and they may be required to name in quick succession the results of each addition as the Inspector or teacher points to the several figures in any order. Oral practice should be given in all the ordinary processes of Arithmetic, and should be so varied as to furnish as many different forms of exercise as possible in concrete as well as in abstract numbers, and in the fractional parts of money, weights and measures. It is often found a help in calculation if the dimensions of the schoolroom, the playground and the desks, and the weight of a few familiar objects are accurately known, and if the figures recording these data are easily accessible and are occasionally referred to as standards of measurement.

Importance of Recitation.—The Recitation of poetry no longer forms a part of English as a Class subject. The usefulness of this exercise as a means of enlarging the range of the scholars' thought, cultivating the imagination and improving the taste, has been so generally recognized, that it has been deemed expedient to retain Recitation as one of the conditions indispensable to the award of the principal grant.

The Study of Thought.—The general object of lessons in English should be to exercise the thinking powers, to enlarge the learner's vocabulary, and to make him familiar with the meaning, the structure, the grammatical and logical relations, and the right use of words. Elementary exercises of this kind have an important practical bearing on everything else which a child learns. From the first, the teaching of the English language should be supplemented by simple exercises in Composition, *e. g.*, when a word is defined, the scholar should be called on to use it in a sentence of his own ; when a grammatical principle is explained he should be asked to frame a sentence showing how it is to be applied, and examples of the way in which adjectives are formed from nouns, or nouns from verbs, by the addition of syllables, should be supplied or selected by the scholars themselves. Mere instruction in the terminology of grammar, unless followed up by practical exercises in the use of language, cannot be expected to yield very satisfactory results.

Geography.—To obtain the mark "good" for Geography the scholars should be required to have prepared three maps, one of which, selected by the Inspector, should be drawn from memory on the day of inspection. Such maps, if of any part of Great Britain and Ireland, should be accompanied by a scale of miles, and if of large and distant countries, by the lines of latitude and longitude. Geographical teaching is sometimes too much restricted to the painting of places on the map, or to the learning by heart of .definitions, statistics, or lists of proper names. Such details, if they form the staple of the instruction, are very barren and uninteresting, Geography, if taught to good purpose, includes also a description of the physical aspects of the countries, and seeks to establish some associations between the names of places and those historical, social, or industrial facts which alone make the names of places worth remembering. It is especially desirable in your examination of the Fourth and higher Standards, that attention should be called to the English Colonies and their productions, government, and resources, and to those climatic and other conditions which render our distant possessions suitable fields for emigration, and for honorable enterprise. In order that the conditions laid down for the geographical teaching of the lower classes may be fulfilled, a globe and good maps both of the country and of the parish or immediate neighborhood in which the school is situated, should form part of the school apparatus, and the exact distances of a few near and familiar places should be known. It is useful to mark on the floor of the schoolroom the meridian line, in order that the points of the compass shall be known in relation to the school itself, as well as on a map."

Character of Elementary Work.—It is not the intention of the Education Department to encourage a pretentious or unreal pursuit of higher studies, or to encroach in any way on the province of secondary education. The course suited to an Elementary school is practically determined by the limit of fourteen years of age, and may properly include whatever subjects can be effectively taught within that limit. It may be hoped that year by year a larger proportion of the children will remain in the Elementary schools until the age of fourteen ; and a scholar who has attended regularly and possesses fair ability may reasonably be expected to acquire in that time not only a serviceable knowledge of Reading, Writing and Arithmetic, of the words he uses, and the world in which he lives, but also enough of the rudiments of two higher subjects to furnish a stable foundation for future improvement. Teachers should not be satisfied unless the instruction in specific subjects awakens in the scholar a desire for further knowledge, and makes him willing to avail himself of such opportunities as are afforded locally by a Science class, a Polytechnic Institute, a course of University Extension lectures, a Free Library or a Home Reading Circle.

Value of Bi-lingual Teaching.—In the case of Wales it is clearly established that in many cases in Welsh-speaking districts the use of Welsh in the school, side by side with English, will greatly facilitate an intelligent understanding of English. It is desirable that the attention of teachers should be called to this question, and that Her Majesty's Inspectors should encourage the practice of bi-lingual teaching by themselves, making use of Welsh in testing children's intelligence. The use of Welsh songs and Welsh poetry in the schools in question will be of considerable service.

General Estimate of the School.—On the occasion of your annual inspection, and especially at a visit without notice, you will endeavor to form an estimate of the tone of the school, the behavior of the scholars, their cleanliness and obedience, their honesty under examination, and especially the degree of interest they show in their work. It will not be difficult for you to judge whether the ordinary discipline of the school is prompt and exact, and is maintained without harshness and without noisy demonstration of authority. The condition of the school furniture and premises, and the proper classification of the scholars for instruction are also matters which require to be considered; and generally it should be borne in mind that the higher grant for discipline and organization should not be recommended unless you are satisfied that the school is a place for the formation of right habits, as well as a place of instruction.

Home Lessons.—Your advice will be occasionally asked respecting Home Lessons, although the subject is mainly one of internal discipline, and not necessarily within your purview. For delicate or very young children such lessons are plainly unsuitable, and the special circumstances of some schools render it inexpedient to require home tasks in any form. Of such circumstances the local managers are the best judges. But in the upper classes of good schools, in which the teachers exert a right influence and take an interest in their work, the practice of giving short exercises to be performed at home is attended with no difficulty, and is open to no practical objection. The best teachers use such exercises rather to illustrate, and to fix in the memory, lessons which have already been explained in school, than to break new ground or to call for new mental effort. This purpose is served by lessons of a very simple and definite character—a sum, a short poetical extract, a list of names or dates, a letter, an outline map, a parsing exercise, such as may readily be prepared in half an hour, and may admit of very easy testing and correction on the following day. When these conditions are fulfilled the home task is found to have a very valuable effect, not only in helping the progress of the scholar, and in encouraging the habit of application, but also in awaking, on the part of the parents, an interest in the school work"

I have given somewhat fully the instructions of the Education Department to the official inspectors, partly because of their value to the corresponding officers in this country, but mainly to show the methods which the Department has approved as the correct one in teaching every subject of the course of study. The rules by which the Inspector is to be guided in his examination of a school will naturally be adopted by the teacher as those most likely to meet with favor, as well as to secure for his pupils a high standing. When inspections are conducted in this thorough manner for a few years, it is quite evident that faulty methods of teaching will soon be corrected and a greater degree of efficiency obtained. The value attached to "recitations" of poetry or prose is worthy of notice. No school that neglects this exercise can receive first-class standing, no matter what may be the attainments of the pupils in other subjects.

The cost of inspection in 1892 was £172,505 14s. 1d. The total expense of the administration of the Department of Education was £232,947 19s. 7d.

From personal observation I may state that the inspection of the English schools is thorough and searching. The Inspector's attitude towards the teacher (and I had several opportunities of observing this), was respectful and considerate, and his manner towards the pupils genial and encouraging. The teachers on the staff appeared to receive him with the greatest pleasure and confidence, and the pupils regarded his inspection without the least fear or agitation. In no case did the imperfections which the Inspector usually discovers excite an unkind remark or a petulant observation. The failure of a pupil to answer a question correctly was treated as an ordinary and not unexpected incident, and where work was well done, the usual encouraging remark, so gratifying to an ambitious pupil, always followed. There was no desire apparently to embarrass the pupil by perplexing or technical questions. Answers that were thoughtful and intelligent, even when not correct, appeared to be fully appreciated, and when the Inspector was done with his day's work it was quite evident to all the teachers on the staff that if there were any weak points in the school they were discovered. Among the many causes which have tended to elevate the Elementary Schools of England, I am satisfied that the stimulating, considerate, but thorough examinations by Inspectors such as I saw during my visits, should not be overlooked.

CHAPTER VI.

SECONDARY SCHOOLS.

Historical Sketch—Classes of Secondary Schools—Public Schools—Courses of Study—Westminster—Winchester—Eton—Rugby—Games and Sports—Value of Discipline—Grammar Schools—Proprietary Schools—Charity Schools—Lord Taunton's Report—Endowed Schools—Prof. Bryce on Training of Teachers in Secondary Schools—Value of Secondary Education.

There are no Secondary Schools in England corresponding to the High Schools and Collegiate Institutes of the Province of Ontario. True, there are schools which provide a full course of instructions in Mathematics and in Classics and Modern languages, but such schools have no organic connection with the Elementary Schools beneath them or with the Universities above them. There is no standard either of age or attainments for admission; they are not subject to Government inspection; they receive no Government aid and their curriculum of studies is as varied as the ideas of their head masters and patrons with regard to what constitutes higher education.

For convenience the Secondary Schools of England may be divided into three classes, Public Schools, Grammar Schools and Proprietary Schools. In Ontario, the term—Public School—applies exclusively to a school in which an elementary education is obtained. In England, the term is not strictly limited as to its meaning. Public School usually means one of the great boarding schools at which boys between the ages of ten and nineteen are placed in residence and fitted for the public service or for matriculation into a University.

Without pretending to be strictly accurate as to the number of schools to which the term "Public School" strictly applies the following may be considered as having an indisputable title to that distinction, viz., Winchester founded in 1387; Eton, in 1441; Shrewsbury, in 1551; Westminster, in 1560; Rugby, in 1567; Harrow, in 1571; and Charterhouse, in 1609. All of these have a long and honorable history, have educated many of England's greatest men, and are still patronized by the rank and wealth of the country. They each have from four hundred to one thousand boys on their rolls. The course of education is classical, at least three-fourths of their energies being devoted to Greek and Latin. They are all boarding schools and while each has its own separate traditions and customs, life at all of them runs largely in the same grooves. Upper Canada College represents this class of schools in the Province of Ontario. The fee at such schools ranges from £100 to £200.

Each of these Public Schools has its own class of patrons and its peculiar traditions. For instance, Westminster was originally the court school. Situated close to the abbey, it was supposed to be under the special protection of royalty and enjoyed a high degree of favor under Elizabeth and the Stuarts. It is said that Dr. Buzby, head master in the time of Charles II. refused to take off his hat in the presence of that monarch as he did not wish his boys to know that there was anyone in the kingdom greater than himself, and the good-natured monarch acquiesced in the arrangement.

Winchester, the oldest of English schools, is patronized by gentry, clergy and professional men. It has retained this characteristic from the first, never having been a court or society school. In scholarship it ranks high and its popularity is indicated by the rule that no boy will be enrolled more than four years in advance of the time he expects to attend.

The "scholars" live in the old quarters, the other boys occupying masters' houses. The "Scholars" take their meals off wooden tables which have come down from the founders' time, use square wooden trenchers instead of plates, and as of old, all the remains go into a tub for the poor of the town.

The charges for instruction are :

1. Upon admission to the school, an entrance fee of £12.
2. For school fees, an annual sum of £33 10s.
3. For board and private instruction by the house master, an annual sum of £78 10s.
4. For medical attendance, 2 guineas.
5. For the gymnasium, 1 guinea.
6. For the infirmary, an annual sum of £1 10s.

Lessons on any subject which do not form part of the teaching of the class in which a boy may for the time being, be placed, are charged for, by arrangement with the house master, subject to the approval of the head master. The school has several valuable scholarships and exhibitions.

Eton, as already stated, was founded in 1441, and was originally intended as a college for priests and for poor boys. Provision was made for seventy boys, all of whom were to be fed and clothed as well as educated, free of charge. Until about forty years ago, the education at Eton was exclusively devoted to the study of the ancient languages of Greece and Rome. Mathematics was not compulsory till 1851. French followed some twenty years later, and Natural Science and German have only recently had a place on the programme. At the present time at least three-fourths of the time af students is given to Greek and Latin. Perhaps not one of the great English schools is regarded by its pupils in after life with so much enthusiasm as Eton, partly because of the distinguished names to be found upon the College rolls and partly because of the delightful situation of the school.

" In London, life is endurable, at the University it was enjoyable, at Eton it was fascinating," said an old Etonian. "And even a stranger wandering over the great meadow play-ground, among the giant elms, noticing the beautiful river winding by, the stately towers of Windsor on the adjacent heights, seeing the ample provision for cricket, boating, fives, racquets, foot-ball, hunting military manœuvres, and gymnastics, thinking of the magnificent history the school has had, the great men who have spent their boyhood there, and whose spirit and pen-knife marks still remain, the old customs which leave their impress on the boys, so that every Etonian has well defined characteristics, can understand the reasons which would induce an old scholar to send his boy to a school to which he would look with so much pleasure in the retrospect. Eton would flourish were its intellectual life very commonplace."

"For some reasons Etonians came to the front in after life. This may be partly explained by the fact that they are born with all the advantages of wealth and inherited position, and are frequently eldest sons. But the school claims, and probably justly, that its own peculiar system encourages and builds up the qualities which make rulers of men. "Waterloo was won on the play-grounds of Eton" said Wellington; and the names of Chatham, Fox, Canning, Peel, and Gladstone bring out her claims in strong light. A recent historian says: "Eton has a special faculty in producing men with the qualities of leadership. She breeds leaders. Go to the Universities and to Sandhurst; explore the army, the Church, the civil service, and the Houses of Parliament; read of enterprize in the colonies and in India; and, in a word, ransack the world of action, and you will find Etonians constantly in the front And, what is more notable, you will observe that these men are not intellectually superior to those they lead. Indeed, they are often inferior. But somehow, they get to the top."

"In so far as school arrangements produce this result, it is probably due to the fact that the initiative is taken in all games and debating societies by the boys. While the masters join, it is only for good fellowship, and not to control in the slightest degree. Much liberty is allowed to a boy in his studies, if only the results are satisfactory. He can largely work alone or can have as good assistance as he wishes. The school is evidently for the boys. They manage it to a large extent, the masters being advisers, with plenty of authority in cases of necessity.

"Eton, in common with some other public schools, has officers called tutors with somewhat peculiar duties. A tutor does not mean a teacher, but a sort of tribune for the boys under his care. Every boy must select one, and retain him during the whole of his school life. The boy has different masters, but always the same tutor. This tutor is to be to him a confidential adviser and friend. If he needs discipline, the offence and the punishment meted out by another master must be reported to the tutor. No one else can report him to the head master. If he is dilatory or in any general way unsatisfactory the tutor will take him in hand. He is strictly *in loco parentis* during the boy's school life.

"The boys live in houses of the masters, about thirty-five in a house. If a house master is also a classical master, he is usually the tutor to the boys who live with him. A mathmetical master cannot be a tutor, nor can a science master or a French or a German master, and if he have boys in his house they must find their tutors elsewhere. The collegers living in college halls have also to select their tutors outside their houses.

Rugby owes much of its popularity to Dr. Thomas Arnold who it is said, revolutionized not only Rugby but also the whole system of public school instruction in

England. Dr Arnold found Rugby discredited partly on account of the laxity of its discipline and of the weakness of its administration. Instead, however, of resorting to the usual modes of punishment to enforce discipline, Dr. Arnold believed and acted out the belief, that boys should govern thmselves, and he rigidly held his sixth form responsible for the conduct of the school. This feeling of responsibility he believed would promote good order and be of substantial benefit to the boys themselves. He encouraged all sorts of manly games and entered heartily into the moral and spiritual lives of his boys and made them feel the power and strength of that interest. Dr. Arnold also led the movement against the exclusive classicism of the schools. He taught his boys to study things as well as words. Although a classical scholar himself, he saw that there was much in nature and humanity well worth the thought and interest of students, and he encouraged the introduction into his curriculum of mathematics, science, history and politics.

"In speaking of the public schools as being mainly classical, it would not be right to infer that provision is not being made for science. Drawing is taught well in all of them. New and convenient chemical laboratories, largely used, are very common. Many have excellent museums, archæological, biological, and geological. Art also is taught with great success. On the modern side, and among certain students of the classicial, remarkably good mathematical results are obtained. Indeed, there are now at the best schools excellent facilities, both in men and equipment, for an ambitious student to work at almost anything he ought to work at. The preponderance of classics is shown in the greater time given to them in the *regular* course and the greater honors allowed to the classical masters over the mathematical, scientific, and modern in almost all the schools."

"The amount of time given to study by the boys, and the zeal displayed in securing intellectual development, probably vary considerably in the different schools. Where a young man knows that his fortune is secure, a powerful incentive to self-sacrificing labor is withdrawn. It is the misfortune of some of the English Public Schools that they have a considerable number of this class, and under these circumstances no official requirement can secure the best results. The penalty most relied on is " superannuation "—dropping a boy from the school if he does not reach a certain form by a certain age. But it is evident this would have no terrors for a "clever" boy, as the English express it, for the penalty has to be modified so as to cover rather flagrant cases only. "Caning" is still occasionally resorted to, and "impositions" of verse-copying etc., are used to prod up dilatory boys. The tutor or house master can also exert much personal influence.

Another remarkable feature of the English Public Schools is the enthusiasm with which all the pupils enter upon all games and sports sanctioned by school authorities so that now such sports are practically compulsory and as much a part of the daily programme as dinner or class-room exercises.

"It is not only ordered that the boy shall play, but what he shall play. Thus in the fall term foot-ball is played universally, and in the spring term cricket. In the winter there is more divergence—racquets, fives, hockey, runs over the country, and a variety of other devices are employed to fill in the programme for three or four days of the week, while rowing comes in more or less all the time where the school is situated so as to admit of it. If it is objected that compulsion would diminish the boys' interest in the game, the answer is that it does not seem to. Very few boys need any compulsion at first, and the number lessens as the term advances.

"An observer whose knowledge of games is intimate and whose sight is keen can not but be struck with the high standard that prevails regarding observance of rules, cheerful submission to the decisions of umpires, and recognition of merit in opponents. After watching many games of foot-ball—the game above all others where temptations to unfair playing are the greatest, and where decisions have to be made quickly and on a very slight preponderance of chances—and after talking to many masters and boys, I have not seen or heard of anything like dishonesty or charges of it; any question of the absolutely correct motives which influenced an umpire's decision, though in some cases he was supposed to have erred in judgment; any unwillingness to accept defeat gracefully and to accord to the opposing victors hearty congratulations; anything, in short, which would make the participants other than better morally for the contest. It is not a proper thing shrewdly to overreach an opponent; it is *ungentlemanly*, and, in the face of public opinion in an English school, no boy would care to have this epithet applied to him.—[Mr. Sharpless' report.]

To keep up an efficient executive management of the vast number of athletic associations in an English school is no slight exercise in business. Funds have to be collected and disbursed; officers elected, and their doings checked and critcised, teams chosen and drilled; and the relations of one association to another have to be determined to the satisfaction of both. All of this is highly useful to citizens of a democratic country.

The governing bodies and the head masters recognize these advantages, and do not confine their actions to merely enforcing attendance. They supply ample grounds; collect the fees from the boys, which go to hire professionals and to keep the grounds in perfect order; select their undermasters quite as much with reference to their athletic as their intellectual prowess; cheer on the boys during the games and after a victory; and show them how to stand a defeat and be the better for it should it come.

This united feeling concerning games makes united feeling in other matters. It creates an open mind and heart to counsel and advice from the masters in matters of deeper import, and is an untold source of influence and power to the officer.

" Great importance is also attached to the formative influence on a boy's character by the continued residence at a Public School. Not only has he at his back the stimulating effects of the traditions of the school but he is under rigid discipline with regard to hours of rising and retiring, hours of study in the class room and hours for private study as well. Being removed from the destructive influences of the social life peculiar to his home, habits of order and self-restraint are developed and although he may not make as rapid progress in his studies perhaps as in a day school, the incidental advantages of residence, with all its opportunities for the development of character, more than compensate for the loss, if any, on the side of rapid intellectual growth. The system of Government which prevails accustoms the boys to rule as well as to submit to the authority of the masters of the school. The sixth form boys are expected to manage all ordinary cases of disorder. They preserve quiet in the dormitories; they see that no bullying of little boys takes place on the play grounds or elsewhere, and that the rules of the school are generally observed. Fagging still prevails to a certain extent. In most schools the little boys run errands for the big ones, do little chores in their rooms, bring up the balls when they go outside the boundaries, and perform numerous services, some menial in their character but on the whole said to be neither difficult nor degrading. The privilege of having a "fag" is limited to the older boys who have been at the school four or five years. The religious influences of such schools are said to be invaluable. As the schools are nearly all connected with the established church the head master is usually a clergyman. The Church catechism is taught as part of the weekly programme and the church order is observed in the daily chapel exercises.

"It is to these and perhaps other influences that the Englishman points when, in spite of some weakness in the way of the acquisition of knowledge, he wishes to justify his confidence in the public schools. He claims that if they do not make as many great scholars, or do not develop all their boys as rapidly as schools of other nations, they do produce something better than great scholarship. They simultaneously cultivate body and mind, force of character, ability to work with men, and moral strength. He claims the qualities which make England great, which characterize Englishmen in the eyes of the world, are the qualities which the public schools beget. He claims that at the end of the course the boys are not intellectually crammed to sickness and surfeit, that the advantage that the French boy has at eighteen is often lost at twenty-five, and that in the case of those boys who can never be scholars, the qualities which go to make strong, self-reliant, forceful men are there instilled, so that a public school boy can be always known in the universities and in the world."

It is not necessary to refer in detail to the other large Public Schools as they all partake more or less of the characteristics of Westminster, Eton and Rugby. They are provided with play grounds and with accommodation for the lodging of either the whole or part of their pupils, and they all claim, and rightly too, to have contributed much to the higher education of the people of England.

Grammar Schools.—As already stated, the line between the Public Schools and the Grammar Schools is not very clearly defined. As a rule the fees for admission to the Grammar Schools are lower than at any of the large Public Schools and on that account they draw their pupils from what are known as the middle classes. There is no limit to the age at which pupils are admitted and like the Public Schools they are not bound by a fixed curriculum nor subjected to inspection by the State. As they receive no State aid they are obliged to depend for their existence partly upon the slender endowments under which they were founded but mainly upon the fees of pupils. The effect of this is practically to exclude the children of the poorer classes who are now receiving a liberal education in the Elementary Schools and whose means will not permit of their paying £20 to £30 a year for admission to the Grammar School and as pupils cannot prepare themselves in the Elementary Schools for matriculation into the University, the privileges of a University course are thus monopolized by the middle and upper classes. It is said that only one per cent. of the whole body of students at the two great universities of England—Oxford and Cambridge—came up from the Elementary Schools and these have worked their way by the aid of scholarships and exhibitions at public examinations. When it is stated that of all the children attending the schools of England and Wales but one per cent. of their whole number are sent to the great universities while the remaining 99 per cent. are sent by the Public or Grammar Schools, the formidable character of the difficulties in the way of the higher education of the people of England becomes apparent. In striking contrast with this exclusiveness is the liberality of our own school system. With us the Public School prepares free of charge, for the High School to which there is no barrier, practically, except that of qualification. The High School prepares for the University under conditions almost equally as favorable and in this why draws its pupils by a process doubtly sifted from all classes of the community irrespective of rank or tradition.

It must not be assumed, however, from these observations that the provision for the higher education of the people of England is inadequate. Her Secondary Schools, as already shown, are generally of a very high grade. what is wanted is not so much an increase in their number, as their re-organization and their recognition as a substantial factor in the educational appliances of the nation. To this end Matthew Arnold, in the last report which he submitted on the subject of education, strongly urged the authorities to organize their Secondary Schools. He says: "The existing resources for secondary education, if judiciously co-ordered and utilized, would prove to be immense; but undoubtedly gaps would have to be filled, an annual state grant and municipal grants would be necessary—that is to say, the nation would perform as a corporate and co-operative work, a work which is now never conceived and laid out as a whole, but is done spasmodically, precariously, and insufficiently. We have had experience how elementary education gains by being thus conceived and laid out, instead of being left to individual adventure or individual benevolence. The middle class, who contribute so immense a share of the cost incurred for the public institution of Elementary Schools while their own school supply is so miserable, would be repaid twenty times over for their share of the additional cost of publicly instituting secondary instruction by the direct benefit which they and theirs would get from its system of schools. The upper class, which has bought out the middle class at so many of the great foundation schools designed for its benefit, and which has monopolized what good secondary instruction we have, owes to the middle class the reparation of contributing to a public system of Secondary Schools."

Proprietary Schools.—A class of schools known as Proprietary Schools is of more recent origin than either of those previously mentioned. These schools are established principally by capitalists in London and some of the other larger cities, as a financial venture. They are necessarily more modern in their methods of instruction, but, like the others, are independent of Government control and impose such fees and employ teachers at such salaries as will enable the stockholders to declare a dividend if at all possible.

Charity Schools,—Besides these three classes of schools whose main object is the preparation of boys for the public service and for the universities, schools known as Charity Schools, for the education of the poorer classes, were founded at different periods in the sixteenth and seventeenth centuries.

The Charity School children were to be taught the Church Catechism, Reading and Writing, and in a few cases, Arithmetic, but were to be sedulously discouraged from attempting to learn more. They were to be clothed in a distinctive dress so as to show that they were objects of public benevolence and to remind them of their rank. It is to be observed that while schools of the charity class were open to girls, the whole of the Grammar School education was provided for boys only. There is scarcely a record in all the voluminous reports of later charity commissions of any school whose founder deliberately contemplated a liberal education for girls; certainly not one who fulfilled such a purpose whether it was contemplated by the founder or not. A girl was not expected "to serve God or the State," and was therefore not invited to the university and Grammar School, but she might be allowed to enter a school as an apprentice or servant, and thereafter the Charity Schools were open to her.

The general spirit of inquiry which was evoked by Lord Brougham and by different Commissions on elementary education, led to inquiries with regard to the efficiency of the Secondary Schools. The peculiar nature of the endowments with which some of them were invested, and the privileges with which they are hedged in were considered unsuitable for a condition of society, entirely different from that which existed at the date of their establishment. It was even alleged that the purposes for which they were founded were not being realized and that it was the duty of the state to see that the intention of their founders was not thwarted by the trustees primarily responsible for the manner in which they were carried on. It was also alleged that some of the conditions under which they were established were incompatible with the best interests of those for whom they were provided, and accordingly a Royal Commission under the presidency of Lord Taunton was appointed to investigate the whole system of secondary education and report to the House of Commons at its earliest convenience. The report of the Commissioners, as was expected by many, showed their condition to be of the most lamentable character. A small number was found to be vigorous, well trained and useful, but in the enormous majority of cases the schools were languishing and inefficient, even more so than ordinary Elementary Schools under inspection. Their failure was attributed (1) To the constitution of the governing bodies, many of which were exclusive cliques, re-united by co-operation and completely out of sympathy with the communities for whom the schools have been designated; (2) to the obsolete and unworkable character of the ancient statutes and to the difficulty experienced by trustees either in carrying them out or in disregarding them; (3) to the fixed or freehold tenure of the head master, and to the conditions under which teachers were appointed; (4) To the general unsuitableness of the instruction given; (5) to the absence of all publicity and supervision; and (6) to the capricious institution of the endowment, the richest often being situated in places where they were least needed, and places of industry being often without endowment.

In their report the Commissioners considered the whole field of secondary education and their observations on the courses of study and the administration of Secondary Schools are of special value, particularly when I mention that such educators as Matthew Arnold, Professor Bryce and Dr. Fitch acted as Assistant Commissioners and had much to do with the preparation of the report which was afterwards submitted to Parliament.

We are sometimes told in Ontario that both our Public and High School are not sufficiently practical, and that greater attention should be paid to studies which directly prepare the pupil for the ordinary callings of life. After full enquiry from the best teachers in England, the commissioners said "special preparation for employment was almost universally condemned as a mistake. It disorganized and broke up the teaching. It conferred a transitory instead of a permanent benefit, since the boy whose powers of mind had been carefully trained speedily made up for special deficiencies, and very often it taught what soon had to be unlearnt and learnt over again."

"In the curriculum of all Secondary Schools alike three leading subjects should be used as the chief instruments for the discipline of the mind: language, mathematics, and physical science. The Commissioners inclined to the opinion that language was the most valuable instrument of the three. 'Nothing,' they say, appears to develop and discipline the whole man so much as the study which assists the learner to understand the thoughts, to enter into the feelings, to appreciate the moral judgments of others. There is nothing so opposed to true cultivation, nothing so unreasonable, as excessive narrowness of mind, and nothing contributes to remove this narrowness so much as that clear understanding of language which lays open the thoughts of others to ready appreciation. Nor is equal clearness of thought to be obtained in any other way. Clearness of thought is bound up with clearness of language, and the one is impossible without the other. When the study of language can be followed by that of literature, not only breadth and clearness, but refinement becomes attainable. The study of history in the full sense belongs to a somewhat later age; for till the learner is old enough to have some appreciation of politics, he is not capable of grasping the meaning of what he studies. But both literature and history do but carry on that which the study of language has begun, the cultivation of all those faculties by which man has contact with man.'"

Among languages, Greek could not be taught with advantage, except in first-grade schools. But Latin could, they thought, be taught with effect in other schools, and Latin held its ground against all other languages, English included, by its character as a language, and by the help it gave in acquiring a scholarly understanding of English, and in learning other languages at the same time or afterwards. Languages, therefore, including, along with Latin, French or German or both, should divide with science and mathematics the chief part of the school time of boys who had first mastered the indispensable elementary subjects. English literature and history should receive careful attention, but they had subordinate claims on the time of the school. Science teaching could best be made a valuable discipline if it began with sciences which appealed at first chiefly to the faculties of simple observation, such as elementary botany, going on to physical geography as a subject which led to some general understanding of natural objects, and ending with elementary chemistry and physics, as " the common groundwork of all the sciences."

In 1869 Mr. Forster introduced into Parliament a bill known as the Endowed Schools Act, some of the provisions of which became law. Under this Bill, a special executive commission was formed, with power to frame schemes for the re-organization of all endowed educational charities, and, with the consent of the local trustees, to apply certain non-educational endowments to educational purposes. Under this Act nearly every educational foundation in England has been subjected to a beneficent, though, in some respects, a drastic revision, and placed on a more substantial basis.

Many of the duties imposed upon the Commissioners under the Forster Act of 1869 and its amendments have been transferred to the Charity Commission. The duty of the Commission is to examine into the nature of the endowments of the Secondary Schools and the statutes under which they are conducted, and so modify their administration as to make them more effective and useful. The managers of many of these schools, to secure the confidence of the people, voluntarily submit the work of the teachers and pupils to the inspection of persons appointed by the Universities of Oxford and Cambridge, the College of Preceptors and the Science and Art Department. It is felt, however, so long as there is no standard of qualification, the highest degree of efficiency cannot be obtained. On this point Professor Bryce, in his introduction to "Studies in Secondary Education," which the Hon. Arthur Acland, Vice-President of the Committee of Council on Education, was good enough to place in my hands, says :

"It is hardly necessary to observe that the greatest advance of all would be to secure teachers of a higher level of ability and skill. Knowledge and skill, however, may be sensibly improved by better provision than has yet been made for the general and professional training of teachers. We may overrate the importance of educational machinery, we may expect too much from modernized curricula; we cannot overrate the excellence of the teacher or spend too much time in endeavoring to secure it. With good teachers nearly everything will have been gained; without them, hardly anything."

The importance attached by Professor Bryce to the training of secondary teachers is a very gratifying endorsation of the policy pursued by the Education Department in the establishment of the School of Pedagogy. No one now expresses any doubt with regard to the usefulness of Normal Schools for the training of elementary teachers. To provide for the training of teachers in Secondary Schools was a declaration in favor of professional culture, to which some objected at the time and perhaps object still. Germany, which has led so intelligently in almost every department of Pedagogics, set an example to the world in that respect. That example Ontario followed in 1885, and the Legislature of New York in 1891, and in 1892 Professor Bryce indicated the necessity of adopting some measure for securing the professional training of the teachers of the Secondary Schools in England.

Although there are many difficulties to be overcome before the Secondary Schools of England are properly organized, it is quite evident, from the progress of the last few years and from the character and standing of the men who are now grappling with the question, that an early solution will be found. On this point I quote with sympathetic pleasure the words of Professor Bryce as not only expressing his own convictions with regard to secondary education in England but also expressing, perhaps not with the same intensity, however, my own experience in the same department of reform:

" A word remains to be said upon the greatest difficulty which the reformers of secondary education have to confront. It is the apathy of the public. One may always count on a widespread interest in the improvement of Primary Schools, because all the world sees that universal education is needed in a democratic country, because an immense number of people occupy themselves as school managers and members of School Boards, and because politicians are anxious to please, or to be seen to wish to please, the mass of the voters. At the other end of the scale one may also count upon some amount of interest in university questions, because the leading men and the leading classes are directly connected with the great universities and colleges, or send their sons to them. Meanwhile the intermediate schools are neglected, and the importance of intermediate education is ignored. No Minister expects to earn gratitude for himself or win credit for his party by dealing with problems whose significance few people perceive; and thus it happens that year after year this whole class of educational reforms is thrust aside. Yet how much of the prosperity and strength and happiness of every civilized country depends upon the excellence of its secondary teaching! What can be more useful to the State than to develop, by the best training, he talent of the most promising youth, passing on the ability and industry of the workingman's child into the

Secondary School, and thence to the university or the technical institute ? What contributes more to the efficiency of professional men than thoroughness of preparation in a Secondary School ? What does so much to raise the general intellectual level of a nation as the enlargement of the minds and the enrichment of the tastes of those large classes who are not wholly absorbed in daily toil, but have, or can have if they wish it, opportunities comparatively ample for cultivating a higher life ? If, in this respect, the professional, and still more the commercial classes—take them all in all—have not reached a level proportioned to the wealth and greatness of England and to the abundance of force and ambition among her people, it is chiefly in the deficiencies of our secondary education that the cause is to be sought."

CHAPTER VII.

GERMAN SCHOOLS.

Organization—Historical Sketch Compulsory Education —Statistics of Attendance—Classification of Schools— Elementary Schools—Instruction in Science—Course of Study — Religious Instruction — Continuation Schools and Private Schools.

The German Empire as such has no Public School system. All public educational institutions in Germany are founded and maintained by the separate and free States which constitute the Empire, or are the result of corporate efforts. Each ingdom, Duchy, Principality, and free State in Germany has its own system of education, just as each State of the United States or each Province of the Dominion determines for itself how its schools shall be organized.

In Prussia the head of the school system is called Minister of Instruction, or more properly speaking, Minister of Spiritual, Educational and Medicinal affairs.

He is a member of the Government, and has representatives and advisers (all together being called the *Ministerium*), an under-secretary and a number of councillors who constitute four distinct councils, one council having charge of church affairs, another medical affairs, and a third matters relating to the universities, art and higher institutions of learning, and a fourth, matters relating to Normal Schools and people's schools. The councillors are skilled men; one for universities; three— one of whom is a Catholic—for higher institutions; and three—one of whom is a Catholic—for normal and people's schools. Immediately under the Ministerium are the universities, technological schools, commission for examining teachers of higher institutions, and other commissions for the normal gymnastic institutes, art academies and the great art collections, etc. Towards all other schools the control of the State is exercised through Provincial Boards. There is also a system of local administration, having to do with the repairs of school buildings and the regulation of the local interests of the school.

In the observations which follow, the schools of Prussia are taken as a type of the German system of education. The variations from this type which prevail in other parts of the German Empire are mere matters of detail, and do not affect the leading features of the system as a whole.

Historical Sketch.—Early in the sixteenth century, efforts were made at the time of the great Church Reformation (A.D. 1517) to reach the masses of the German people by the establishment of schools for the lower classes of society. These schools, which at first were open only on Sunday, were afterwards extended to week days, and were supported by the communities and by tuition fees. Under Frederick the Great of Prussia, an effort was made to extend this system to the whole of Prussia, and these efforts have been continued with laudable enthusiasm by his successors. The practical organization of German elementary schools, however, in their present form, may be said to have commenced with the Prussian Code of Regulations issued in October, 1854. As evidence of the importance attached by the people to the education of the masses, the following quotations from the Constitution of Prussia may be cited :—

Article 20.—Science and the teaching of science are free.

Article 21.—For the education of the young, public schools shall be established and maintained. Parents and guardians must not leave their children or wards without that instruction that is provided for the public schools.

Article 23.—All public and private educational institutions are under the supervision of the State authorities. Teachers of public schools have the rights and duties of officers of the State (in this clause the State reserves for itself the right of properly preparing the teachers, and assumes the duty of pensioning them).

Article 24.—The external maintenance of schools is left to the civil communities, while the State employs the teachers and provides for the necessary number and training of teachers.

Article 25.—The means for establishing, maintaining and extending the public school system are furnished by the communities, and only in case of inability does the State furnish the means. The State guarantees public school teachers a fixed income. Instruction in the public schools is free of charge.

Notwithstanding the obligation placed upon the communities to maintain public schools, the State provides 18 per cent. of the cost of maintaining Elementary Schools and about 34 per cent. of the cost of secondary education. Although, theoretically, the public schools are free, still in the majority of the communities, fees as a rule very moderate in their amount, are still charged. Berlin, Frankfort and several other of the larger cities have abolished fees altogether, and provide for the maintenance of the schools by direct taxation. The contributions of the State are not based on average attendance as in Canada, nor upon a combination of average attendance and efficiency, as in England, but upon the teaching staff employed. For each principal an annual grant of $100 is given, for each regular teacher $50, for each female teacher $37.50 and for temporary assistants $25. The support of the Elementary Schools is considered a most important duty of the State. Even in time of war the schools must not be closed. The teachers who have passed the final examination and receive definite appointments are sure of their pay, even though the schools to which they are appointed cease to exist. Teachers in Elementary Schools are on the same footing with clergymen as regards freedom from the payment of taxes. They have but six weeks instead of three years' military service, and for this time their wages as teachers, and those of their substitutes as well, must be paid. They are also freed from the duty of quartering soldiers in time of war, and at the close of their active service they draw a pension from the Government.

Compulsory Education.—Every Prussian child between the ages of six and fourteen years must, except in case of severe illness, or other extraordinary cause, be present at every session of the school he attends. The list of the children of school age in charge of the local police is kept so carefully that it is as difficult to escape the provisions of the compulsory education laws as to evade the military service. Dispensation amounting to more than four weeks in the school year is given only to children under twelve years of age, and to them only when sickness in the family or other unusual cause makes it advisable; and in order to guard children from the avarice of their parents or guardians, those under twelve years of age are forbidden to work in factories or mines, and those between twelve and fourteen are restricted by law to six hours' work per day. Examinations are held regularly to determine the pupils' attainments, and they may be forced to attend school beyond the close of the fourteenth year when through previous irregular attendance or lack of diligence the results of the examination are not satisfactory. Pupils leaving Elementary Schools before the close of the fourteenth year to attend a higher school must submit to the school commissioner a certificate from the director of such higher school. In every province there are houses of correction for children of school age who cannot be otherwise controlled. In 1885 there were 180 such houses, to which 11,101 children were sent during the seven previous years. That compulsory education has been effective is seen from the fact that for some years the average number of recruits to the army without Elementary School training has not exceeded 2 per cent., and in many parts of the kingdom has been less than one-fifth of 1 per cent.

Although truants are wrought upon in all possible ways, even to being sent to a reformatory or school of correction, as stated, the parents or guardians are generally held accountable for their children's absence from school, and are punished with fines or imprisonment for a violation of the law. In Prussia a parent or guardian is fined from 10 pfennings ($2\frac{1}{2}$ cents) to a mark (25 cents) for each day of his child's unexcused absence from school, and in case the fine is not paid immediately the parent may be imprisoned from three hours to one day. Instead of imprisonment the parent fined may work the same length of time for the benefit of the Commune. Employers allowing children to work during school hours are fined from one to 150 marks, or imprisoned not exceeding fifteen days. The following statement shows the thoroughness with which the compulsory laws of Prussia are enforced. Although dated 1st December, 1885, I have no doubt, were more recent statistics available, they would be as conclusive:

Whole number of children obliged to attend school	5,333,456
Number in attendance upon public schools	4,838,247
Number in attendance upon private and public schools	299,280
Number of children not yet in the school, or children who have left, all for good reasons,	170,439
Number not in attendance on account of some physical or mental defect	13,519
Number not in attendance for want of room	8,826
Number absent unexcused	3,145

Classification of Schools.—The German system of education is more highly organized and sub-divided into a greater number of classes than the school system of any other country in the world. For convenience, however, it may be considered under the classification best understood in Canada, viz:, Elementary Schools, High Schools and Normal Schools.

Elementary Schools.—The course of the Elementary people's schools (Volkschulen) generally covers a period of eight years. The subjects taught are:—Religion, Language, Reading, Writing, Arithmetic, History or Geography, Object lessons, Natural History, Geometry, Physics, Drawing, Singing, Gymnastics. In cities and large towns it is the almost universal custom to divide the pupils into eight grades, and to place pupils of the same grade in separate rooms. Each grade of pupils is in charge of a teacher who may or may not spend his whole time with them. In some cases schools are conducted on the departmental system and the same teacher is in charge of one subject throughout the whole school. All schools are required to given instruction in religion (including Bible and Church history and the catechism), the average time devoted to this subject in a graded school being about four hours and a quarter per week.

Object lessons are taught to classes during the first three years. Reading, Writing, Arithmetic and Drawing are taught during every year of the course; Natural History, Singing and Gymnastics during the last five years; Geometry and Physics during the last two years. When the number of pupils is too large to be taught by one teacher at a time, or when the conditions are not favorable for two teachers to be employed, half-day schools are formed, the advanced pupils attending forenoons, and the younger pupils attending afternoons.

In most parts of Germany tuition in the elementary schools is free, and text books are provided for all pupils whose parents cannot afford to pay for them.

In the country districts the boys and girls are generally brought together in the same school. In cities the custom is to separate the sexes in all of the upper classes, and in many of the lower classes.

The use of objects and pictures in teaching and in illustrating subjects which are to be presented to a class, is a marked feature of the elementary schools; and in all schools the value of skilful questioning in leading pupils from the known to the unknown seems to be well understood by teachers.

Great attention is paid to Elementary Science in the form of observation lessons. From two to four recitations a week, of nearly an hour each, during the entire course are given to lessons upon plants, animals, minerals, physics, or chemistry. In some schools the observation of plants, animals and minerals, does not begin until the third and fourth years; or, if these objects are observed, it is only in a general way. The following outline shows what is attempted in some schools during the first three years of the course:—

First Year.—Naming and describing objects in the immediate neighborhood; writing clear simple sentences in connection with observation; and, showing the relation of children to parents, to household, to school and to church.

Second Year.—Conversations upon familiar plants, animals and minerals, concerning their uses, etc., in the same manner, the various articles in common use and their manufacture; instruction regarding the treatment of animals and care of plants.

Third Year.—Continuation of animal, plant and mineral lessons; home geography. In the schools working under this and other plans of study, for the first three years there are observed and talked about, in addition to the common plants, animals and minerals, such familiar objects as the stove, the egg, the house, the schoolroom, the bed, clothing, food, the garden, the field.

In other schools and with more advanced pupils a more elaborate study is attempted as follows: —

1. The plant considered by itself.
   (a) Description, root, stem, leaves, blossoms, fruit location and time of blossoming.
   (b) Its life, first appearance, growth, length of life annual or perennial.
2. The plant as a part of nature.
   (a) Relations to soil, moisture, climate; opposing influences.
   (b) Relations to the plants in the neighborhood, growing alone or with other plants; shade; parasites.
3. The plant in relation to man.
   (a) Use; harmful effects of.

In a similar manner animals are studied.

Although these various plans differ in respect to the chief end to be attained, there is no difference of opinion as to the necessity of presenting the objects themselves for study. All insist upon that, and where the objects cannot be conveniently presented, representations of them in various forms are used instead.

The following topical outlines, copied from a special plan of study, indicate the kind of work which is attempted in many schools of Southern Germany, beginning with the fourth year. It should be understood that these topics are placed before the pupils one at a time, as the observations are made or as the information is given :
1. The four fundamental forms of organs (stem, root, leaves and hairs). 2. Functions of these organs. 3. Growth of stems, outer and inner. 4. Underground stems. 5. Above-ground stems. 6. Length of life of stem. 7. Buds, growth, kinds, covering, position, unfolding development, service to the plant. 8. Malformations and diseases of stems. 9. Influence upon the stem of location, soil, light and warmth, height, direction of wind, etc. 10. Growth of root. 11. Kinds of roots. 12. Effects of changing food. 13. Influence of location and soil. 14. Duration of root. 15. Leaves, kinds, etc. 16. Development of leaves. 17. Forms of leaves. 18. Situation of leaves. 19. Cause of malformation and diseases of leaves 20. Influence of food, light, etc., upon the leaves. 21. Blossoms. 22. Corolla. 23. Characteristic forms of blossoms. 24. Essential and unessential parts of flower. 25. Use of flower coverings. 26. Influence of light, moisture, etc., upon the formation of the flower. 27. Structure and use of stamens. 28. Structure and use of pistils. 29. Fertilization. 30. The fruit. 31. Seeds,

structure and germination. 32. Dissemination of fruits and seeds. 33. Influence of location upon quantity of fruit and seeds."

The object of this study appears to be (1) cultivation of the observing faculties; (2) assistance to a better understanding of other studies; (3) acquisition of facts as a basis for scientific study; (4) development of a love of the beautiful in nature and training in ethics.

"In the early object-lessons, as well as in the later ones in natural history, the ethical training of the pupil is one of the distinct objects of the lessons in natural history. For example, in one general plan of study it is stated, after speaking of the obvious purposes of the lessons : 'At the same time there should be given, in a fitting way, the representation and comprehension of the ethical relations of the child to the objects observed and talked about.' Especially is kindness to animals enjoined upon children in all lessons upon the domestic and harmless animals."

A similar course is pursued with regard to the study of physics. The purpose evidently being :—

(1) To direct attention to simple and important facts by the aid of questions.

(2) By practical illustration to explain the character and effect of the laws of matter. Simple appliances and the use of charts and a black-board invariably accompany all lessons of this kind.

The reading books used in the lower grades are also prepared with the view to extend the pupil's knowledge of natural objects. Through all of them there are interspersed selections from the best German authors, and on the whole appear to be compiled from a higher literary standpoint than Canadian text-books in the same subject. They contain fewer of what may be called nursery stories, and to be profitably read, require greater thought on the part of pupils and a higher standard of culture on the part of teachers. Less attention is paid to methods of reading and expression in German schools than to a mastery of thoughts contained in the selection. Every reading lesson is primarly a thought lesson ; secondly, a lesson in literature and language, and thirdly, a lesson in enunciation and expression. Where the selections admit of it the lesson is made the basis of developing that patriotic feeling which so strongly characterizes the German people. Much attention is also paid to the literature of Germany, and pupils are expected to memorize freely from the German poets, especially Goethe and Schiller.

Formal grammar as understood in the schools of Ontario occupies a comparatively humble place in the elementary schools. It must not be supposed, however, that the study of grammatical expression receives no attention. Composition is taught in connection with every reading lesson, and the grammatical errors of pupils during recitation are severely criticized. Three sets of blank books are generally found in every school ; one for penmanship, one for dictation exercises, and one for composition. In the blank book for composition the pupil is expected to enter in his own language the substance of the lesson for the day, and to write from memory the proverbs and sayings learned by heart. In the advanced classes, short themes are written on familiar subjects. At the close of the lesson in natural history, geography, the history of the Fatherland, etc., pupils are expected to write down what they have learned. The writing of all these lessons and the punctuation are carefully criticized, and great attention paid to neatness, arrangement and accuracy of finish. In the upper grades at least one composition a week is required of every pupil. The following rules are the teacher's guide in such an exercise :—

1. See that the pupils have clear ideas of the subject to be treated. The simple compositions are the most instructive.
2. The material should be of every possible kind, including what is observed, told and read.
3. "Practice makes the master." Short original compositions should be called for frequently.
4. The pupil's thought as well as expression should be as original as possible.
5. Simplicity is a proof of clearness of ideas.
6. There should be progressive steps from the simple to the complex; therefore the teacher should have a definite plan laid out for the year.

Geography and History.—In geography and history the pupil is first introduced to the study of the school-house and its surroundings. The general plan being as follows :—

"Conversations upon the town and vicinity. Observation lessons, measuring (by steps) and descriptions of the school-room, the school-house, the yard according to directions (by the sun); observation and description of the nearest surroundings of the school-house, streets and most important buildings, squares, etc.

Drawing of objects that have been observed. The plans at first drawn, with reference to directions, and approximate distances, upon a black-board laid horizontally. Consideration of a plan of the school-house and vicinity. Conversations upon the inhabitants of the town, the number of people and of families, the difference in sex, age, occupations, authority, etc., all being connected with ethical instruction After attention has been given to the town, instruction by observation and descriptions should be extended to the neighborhood. For this purpose visits to the neighboring forests, meadows and fields, should be made—highlands and valleys, ponds and streams of water, should be observed with constant reference to direction, distance, etc. In these observations essential geographical ideas are developed, as of horizon, hill, mountain, mountain-chain, valley, mountain-peak, slopes, foot of the mountain, plain, brook, river, spring, banks, bed, mouth, branches, island, peninsula, lake, sea, bay, etc.

Text-books in geography generally have no maps, and consist of bare outlines and essential facts. The teacher is supposed to give in the recitation all details of information, or to leave the pupils to infer them. At the close of the lesson the pupils copy in their note books the substance of what they were taught. The schools are usually well supplied with maps, charts and geographical apparatus illustrative of physical and mathematical geography. Map drawing and modelling in clay are also practised. Great attention is paid to the geography and topography of Germany, its climatic conditions, the occupation of the people, its natural resources, etc. The study of foreign countries is limited to their general physical features, position, climate and products.

The central point in the teaching of history in all grades of schools is the Fatherland—that is Germany. Whatever can be said of the greatness of Germany and its relations to other countries, is never omitted by the teacher. The lives of her celebrated men, her poets, warriors and scholars, are carefully studied, and the part they played in the history of the German Empire and the history of the world, vividly presented to the pupils, both in connection with the history and the reading lessons.

Drawing is obligatory in all the public elementary schools, and in all or some classes of the High schools. In some schools there are special masters who give their whole time to this subject. In the lower grades drawing is usually taught from copies; in the higher grades, however, models are used. The drawing-books in use in the German schools are in no respect different from those authorized in the Province of Ontario. In the schools of Leipsic, where I examined the subject more particularly, drawing was taught in the elementary classes, as preparatory to the study of drawing from objects. The large supply of plaster-casts of various objects showed the importance attached to the proper development of this subject.

Singing holds a prominent place in the programmes of all grades of schools, and is most carefully and thoroughly taught. In graded schools special teachers are provided, and the use of the organ, violin or piano, is thought necessary to the best work in singing in all grades. In the lower grades singing by note is not practised to any great extent, rote singing of common songs apparently being most favored. In observing the exercises of the pupils, a visitor is at once struck with the sweetness and purity of the tones, with the absence of loudness and harshness, and with the distinct enunciation of the pupils.

Physical Training.—Systematic instruction in gymnastics is made obligatory in the schools of nearly every State. In every graded school in the cities and towns there is generally a room well fitted up with apparatus, and devoted exclusively to physical exercises. The exercises are generally very rigid, with no elements of attraction for children except the natural pleasure derived from bodily movements. The effect of this, with the military drill in after life, has already made its impress upon the German nation.

Religious Instruction.—Religious instruction is given in all schools, both public and private, and, as a rule, is given by the regular teachers, although clergymen are appointed by the Government to teach in some of the higher grades, and in schools where special instruction is needed. The religious belief of a plurality of the parents determines the character of the teaching—whether Protestant, Roman Catholic or Jewish. In some sections twelve or more pupils of the minority may demand special instruction, different from what the plurality receive.

This instruction is given either by special teachers in the school where the pupils are who desire the special instruction, or the pupils may go to another school to receive the desired instruction.

The various courses of study make specific provision for instruction according to Protestant and Roman

Catholic faiths, although only slight differences are observable. There is in both courses provision for learning Bible stories, Bible history, explanations of the Bible and book of worship, and the catechism. The memorizing of passages from the Bible 'and book of worship, and the singing of hymns and chorals, also constitute a part of the religious instruction.

Continuation Schools.—When a pupil completes the course of study at the Elementary Schools, although he passes the age, fourteen years, at which compulsory attendance ceases, his education is not supposed to be at an end. In some parts of Germany, attendance upon Continuation Schools is compulsory for at least two years. These schools like our Canadian Night Schools, receive aid from the Government, and are under the supervision of the school authorities. Their sessions are from two to four hours a week either in the evening or on Sundays, depending upon the location of the school and the time of the year. In most of them, Reading, Writing and Arithmetic are compulsory, although in many places provision is also made for instruction in Natural History, Elementary Science, Geography, History, Physiology, Geometry, Bookkeeping and Drawing. The last two subjects are taught to apprentices and always in reference to their need.

Discipline is maintained as in other schools by the prompt support of boards and judges. The conduct of boys even out of school hours seems to be under the control of the school officials in some places, and boys in attendance at a Continuation School are, in some localities, forbidden under a certain age to smoke or enter a saloon.

The city of Berlin is said to possess the best system of evening and Sunday schools in Germany. In the case of Continuation Schools for girls the curriculum is varied from that already stated so as to include Domestic Economy, Sewing, Embroidery, and Dress Cutting. Nearly all the teachers in these schools are principals and teachers of Day Schools who are paid a special allowance for this class of work.

Private Schools.—Though Germany may be said to have given to the world the Kindergarten system of instruction, strange to say, that system has not been recognized by the State as an integral portion of elementary education. All Kindergartens in Germany are Private Schools, but like all other Private Schools in Germany, are subject to the inspection of the authorities. Indeed, in Prussia and several of the smaller States, no teacher can be employed in a private school or even in a private family, who has not passed certain examinations required by the Government. No Private School can be established until evidence is presented of the intention and ability of its founders to support a school equal in efficiency to public schools of the same kind ; nor where there is already sufficient accommodations in the Public Schools. From what I saw and learned with regard to the Kindergarten in Germany or in England, I am of the opinion that the system as well as the principles which underlie Kindergarten instruction are more closely followed in Ontario than in either of these countries, and that whatever educational value there is in Kindergarten methods, under our organization children profit more from the work of the Kindergarten in Canada than they do in England or in Germany.

Besides the schools whose object is to instruct in some particular industry, and whose support and management falls partly upon private corporations and partly upon the city, there are the following schools, intended to supplement the work of the public day schools:—

(1). Schools whose course is a continuation of a middle or high school course. The subjects of instruction are French, English, German, Mercantile Arithmetic, Book-keeping, Drawing, Natural Science, Commercial Law, and Commercial Geography. There are two terms of twenty weeks each, and the school is in session four evenings in the week and Sunday forenoons. A small fee is charged for tuition, depending upon the number of hours of instruction.

(2). Continuation Schools for boys who have graduated from the public elementary schools. The subjects taught are German, (reading, writing, and language) Arithmetic, and Drawing, and under certain circumstances Book-keeping, Geometry, Physics, Geography, History, Foreign Languages, and Singing. A small fee is charged for advanced studies; for the others the instruction is free. There are two evening sessions of two hours each, and a Sunday session of four hours—forty weeks in the year.

(3). Continuation Schools for girls in which German, Aritmetic, Book-keeping, Drawing, Sewing, Embroidery and Dress-cutting, are taught three evenings a week, and Sunday forenoons. A small tuition fee, from one-half mark to one mark a month, is charged the pupils.

(4). Free Continuation Schools for deaf and dumb, and for the blind ; the common branches only are taught.

(5). Free Schools for youth of both sexes, in which, in addition to the common branches, there is given instruction in special kinds of work, as chimney-sweeping, shoe-making and baking.

The rooms, with heating and lighting, are provided by the city. All other expenses are borne by private associations.

Nearly all the teachers of the above-named schools are principals and teachers of day schools, their salaries ranging from one mark to five marks for each hour's instruction.

CHAPTER VIII.

GERMAN SECONDARY SCHOOLS.

Sketch—Classes of Schools—The Gymnasium—Time Table—Real Schools—Leaving Examination—Examination of Teachers—Probejahr—Appointments—Pensions—Educational Conference, 1890—The Emperor's Speech—Comparison with Ontario.

The Secondary School System of Germany, unlike the English system, is of later origin than the Elementary Schools. Although Germany has had her Universities dating back many centuries, it was not until about the beginning of the present century that decisive steps were taken to organize and develop a system of Secondary education. The determination to rescue the nation from the humiliating position to which it was brought by the success of Napoleon, gave an impulse to Elementary Education. The same determination which induced Frederick William III., in 1807, to say, "the State must make good through intellectual power what it has lost in physical strength," led to the organization of Secondary Schools under Wilhelm von Humboldt as the responsible head of its school system. The three great reforms which he inaugurated, viz., the

State Examination for Teachers, the re-organization of the course of study, and the final examination, justified, the success achieved by the German nation in the astonishing progress which it has made politically and educationally.

The Secondary Schools of Germany are of three different types, corresponding in a general way to the course which a pupil can make for himself by selecting certain optional subjects in our High Schools. In the schools called Gymnasia and Progymnasia, the study of the Classics predominate, and in the Realgymnasium the course is a classical scientific course, and in the Real Schools and higher burgher schools, the courses are scientific. Instead of allowing pupils in the same school by a series of options to select courses suited to their future purpose in life, German High Schools, classified as already mentioned, are established where the desired courses can be obtained, but no school gives more than one course.

The Gymnasium.—The Gymnasium is a classical school par excellence. It has properly six classes from Sexta, the lowest, to Prima, the highest. In the three lower classes the course is one year; in the three upper it is two years, making the entire course nine years. There are two terms, or semesters, in each year. The Progymnasium is simply a Gymnasium which lacks the upper classes, that is, the two years of prima.

A glance at the following Time Table of a Gymnasium shows the relative importance attached by the authorities to the various subjects in the prescribed course of study.

Subjects.	Number of Recitations Weekly.									
	First Year.	Second Year.	Third Year.	Fourth Year.	Fifth Year.	Sixth Year.	Seventh Year.	Eighth Year.	Ninth Year.	Total.
Religion	3	2	2	2	2	2	2	2	2	19
German	3	2	2	2	2	2	2	3	3	21
Latin	9	9	9	9	9	8	8	8	8	77
Greek	....	....	....	7	7	7	7	6	6	40
French	....	4	5	2	2	2	2	2	2	21
History and Geography	3	3	4	3	3	3	3	3	3	28
Mathematics	4	4	4	3	3	4	4	4	4	34
Natural History	2	2	2	2	2	....	....	....	....	10
Physics	....	....	....	....	....	2	2	2	2	8
Writing	2	2	....	....	....	....	....	....	....	4
Drawing	2	2	2	....	....	....	....	....	....	6
Gymnastics	2	2	2	2	2	2	2	2	2	18
Singing	2	2	2	2	2	2	2	2	2	18
Total	32	34	34	34	34	34	34	34	34	304

Hebrew, and, in some schools, English are elective for four years of the course.

From this Time Table it will be seen that Greek is not taken up until the Fourth year, Natural History is dropped at the end of the Fifth year, Physics is not taken up until the Sixth year, Writing is not taken beyond the

Second year, and Drawing not beyond the Third year. It will also be seen that while there are four recitations weekly for Mathematics, and two for Physics, there are nineteen recitations for language. In schools where English takes the place of Greek or Hebrew the average recitation is about three per week. The subject of Greek as a rule is not taken up until the beginning of the Fourth year. The practice recently adopted in Ontario, and which to some extent prevails in the High Schools of the United States, is found in all the German schools, that is to say, minor subjects, such as Penmanship and Drawing, are disposed of in the first year or two of the course. By this means the pupils are free to give all their time and strength to advanced subjects. The foreign languages as a rule, are never begun simultaneously. Latin which is a favorite, is always taken up in the first year along with the mother tongue—German. French is generally taken the second year, and Greek or English the fourth year. Physics and Chemistry are also postponed to the last three years of the course. The only subjects which are carried through the entire course are Religion, German, Latin, History and Geography, Arithmetic, Gymnastics and Singing. In schools intended exclusively for girls more time is given to German and less to Mathematics and English, than in the schools devoted to boys. Graduation from a Gymnasium entitles the student to enter a University.

Real-Schools.—The name *Realschule* or Real-school was first used at Halle. Christopher Semler, in 1738, established there a school with this title. Isolated schools of this type were found in various parts of the country, but they were not successful until about 1822. In 1832 the Government began to occupy itself somewhat with them, and in 1859 a definite plan and course was framed for them, as had previously been done for the Gymnasium. Three kinds of real-schools were distinguished in this Government order of 1859—real-schools of the first rank, real-schools of the second rank, and higher burgher schools. In the words of the decree, all these three classes " have the common purpose of affording a general scientific preparation for those callings for which university studies are not required." Real-schools of the first and second order had, like the Gymnasiums, a nine-years' course; the higher burgher schools, a six-years' course. In real-schools of the first order, Latin was a required study; real-schools of the second order did not have Latin in their course and could adapt themselves more to the local needs. As the terms are at present, used, all the schools except gymnasiums are included under the general name of " real institutions," and give a "realistic" or "scientific and practical" training. Higher real-schools are schools without Latin, having a full nine-years' course. *Real-schools* simply lack the two upper classes of *higher real-schools*. They are seven-class institutions.

The Real Gymnasium.—By a Government order of the 31st of March, 1882, the study plan of the real-schools of the first order was materially modified and the name real-gymnasium was applied to them. This class of schools are therefore now called in Prussia real-gymnasiums, and in the other German States, real-schools of the first order. The change made consisted briefly in increasing the amount of Latin by about 25 per cent.

There are other classes of German schools such as the *Oberrealschulen*, covering a course of nine years, in which Latin is dropped and special attention paid to French, English, Physics, Chemistry, Mathematics and Drawing; *Hohere Burgherschulen* with a six years' course, but in other respects almost similar to the *Oberrealschulen*; *Hohere Madchen Schulen*, with a ten years' course, in which special prominence is given to the study of French, the English language and Literature, Singing, Drawing and Sewing.

Final Examinations.—The final examination in the higher schools, variously called a leaving examination, an examination for maturity, for ripeness, for dismissal, etc., is of the greatest importance to all the pupils. On this examination depend all the privileges which the higher schools confer. Graduates of Gymnasiums have open to them nearly all the posts of honor and profit; they are admitted to the Universities and to the study of any of the learned professions as well as to teaching in all its branches. Graduates of the Real-gymnasiums are excluded from the learned professions and may study only with the philosophical faculty of a University, and may become teachers only in Mathematics and Modern Languages, and are then eligible for positions only in Real-schools. The Real-schools qualify for admission to the technical High Schools.

Under the system of military service prevailing in Germany, every German youth must serve three years in the army. If, however, he has completed six years of the course in the higher schools, that is to say the entire course of a higher burgher school, or the course as far as

Upper Secunda of the Gymnasium, Real-gymnasium or Real-school, one year of military service is all that is required of him.

The final or leaving examination to which so much importance is attached, is both oral and written. The paper work lasts a week. The oral examination is open to the public. The teachers attend in full dress. Each class is examined by its instructor, but the President of the Examining Commission may choose any passage for translation and put any question he thinks proper. Every effort is made to avoid cramming and special preparation, and to make the examination such as " a scholar of fair ability and proper diligence may, at the end of his school course, come to with a quiet mind, and without painful preparatory effort, tending to relaxation and torpor as soon as the examination is over."

Examination of Teachers.—The Staatsprüfung (Government examination,) for teachers in Prussia has long been famous. It originated with Wilhelm von Humboldt and the regulations governing it have been modified from time to time, especially in 1831 and 1866. Before 1810 the method of appointing teachers was very loose. No certificate of fitness to teach was required. Favoritism was the prevailing principle.

The examination at present is held by one of the High Examination Commissions. The candidate must present his certificate for ripeness for University studies and with it the certificate of three years' attendance at University lectures. The examination itself is both oral and written. Fitness to teach in the Gymnasium is the standard set. A special examination is required for teachers in the Real-schools, in Modern Languages, History, Geography, Chemistry, and the descriptive Natural sciences.

The examination refers, first to the candidate's general preparation for the teaching of Philosophy, Pedagogy, History, Geography and Languages. This part may be dispensed with if unusually excellent academic certificates are presented. Second, to the special preparation for the particular branches the candidate wishes to teach. The certificate of fitness to teach, or *facultas docendi*, can be acquired in any one of the four following departments: (1) Philology and History; (2) Mathematics and Science; (3) Religion and Hebrew; (4) Modern Languages. For written examinations every candidate must present a thesis on the general field of Philosophy and Pedagogy, and in addition one or more thesis on his special subject. If that be the classics it must be written in Latin; if modern languages, in the language to which it relates. This thesis may be dispensed with in the case of graduates of the University with the degree of Ph. D. In case the examination is passed the candidate receives a *facultas docendi*, which is conditional or unconditional. There are three grades, the first of which permits him to teach in the higher classes—prima and higher secunda, the second grade in lower secunda and tertia, and the third grade in the lower classes.

Trial Year.—Having passed his examination the candidate is not at once installed in a position, but must first pass through a *Probejahr* or trial year, which has been required since 1826. He is assigned to some Gymnasium or Real-gymnasium, not to the lower school, in order that he may at least become acquainted with the methods in the higher schools, even though his work shall lie afterwards in lower grades. He is under the charge of the director, and teaches from six to eight hours a week. He attends the teachers' conference, visits the various classes, and is given every opportunity to make himself perfectly familiar with his future calling. The director is specially enjoined not to regard the candidate as a means of relieving an overburdened teaching staff. As a rule the candidate receives no pay, but if he is required to do the work of an assistant teacher he is then entitled to corresponding remuneration At the end of the year a report of his work is made out by the director and presented to and approved by the provincial school board.

Appointments.—At the end of his *Probejahr* the candidate gets his appointment. The ordinary teachers are appointed by the provincial board, the higher teachers by the same with the approval of the Minister of Education, and the directors by the Crown, through the ministry in all Crown patronage institutions. In schools of municipal or private patronage, the Crown's assent is required. All directors and teachers, however appointed, are required on installation in office to take the following oath :

I swear to God the Almighty and Omniscient after I have been appointed as   of the   to be submissive, loyal, and obedient to His Royal Majesty of Prussia, my most precious lord to fulfil all the duties obligatory upon me, by virtue of my office, conscientiously and according to my best knowledge, and to faithfully observe the constitution. So help me God.

Material Conditions.—The general scale of salaries is, for directors, from $975 to $1,350 per year; for teachers, from $375 to $975 per year. These figures are supposed to represent the total income; in case a house is provided 10 per cent. is deducted from the salary. There is an ascending scale with length of service. According to the law of the 1st of March, 1833, teachers disabled from further duties receive pensions as follows: For ten years of service, fifteen-sixtieths of the salary with increase of one-sixtieth for each additional year of service until the total reaches forty-five sixtieths. The trial year and time spent in military service is counted towards the pension, and the time spent in the field before the enemy is reckoned double. After the age of 65 all are entitled to pensions and are liable to receive them and be relieved from active service without requesting it. They are not prohibited from holding another employment along with their school posts, but must get permission to do so, and it must be such as not to interfere with their school duties. They are at liberty to give private instruction as much as they please. They are almost absolutely secure in their positions. The authority of the ministry extends no further than reprimanding and stopping a month's salary. The directors and higher teachers are under the jurisdiction of the court of discipline for the civil service at Berlin, a judicial body composed partly of members of the supreme court. Any complaints regarding the dismissal of a director or higher teacher must be tried before it. From the sentence of the court there is an appeal to the minister, who must appoint two referees, one a member of the department of justice, to hear the appeal, and their decision is final. Complaints involving the dismissal of ordinary teachers are tried by the provincial school board acting as a court. From the sentence of a board there is an appeal to the minister, who appoints one referee, and the referee, before deciding, must take the opinion of the court of discipline.

One of the most remarkable events in the history of modern German education was the great educational conference, held at Berlin, on the 4th of December, 1890. The conference was composed of educationists of the highest standing and was presided over by Von Gossler, Minister of Instruction. An address by the Emperor was one of the interesting features. The object of the conference was to consider:—

(1) The position which instruction in religion should occupy in the German system of education.

(2) The extent to which the history of the Fatherland might be used for developing a greater interest in "a regulated government with a secure monarchical direction for the protection and prosperity of the individual in his civil and industrial relations" with a view to counteracting socialism.

(3) A consideration of the best means for qualifying teachers for their professional duties.

The Emperor in his address strongly attacked the socialistic tendencies of the times, asserting that if the course of instruction in the higher schools was more national and less literary and classical the socialistic spirit would soon die out. He argued in favor of a better acquaintance with German history and and the German language, of a reduction in the amount of classical instruction required in the gymnasium and greater attention to physical exercises and gymnastics. He also advocated the better training of teachers and the simplification of the school curriculum generally.

The discussions of the conference are of great value to educators as showing particularly the importance attached by the best scholars and teachers in Germany to the study of the classics as a preparation for professional and public life and as also showing the importance which was attached to the personality of the teacher in the school-room. On the latter point the conference favored "the teacher remaining with his classes as long as they are in in the school-room, giving instruction in all branches of study and maintaining the entire discipline, on the ground of the superior influence that could thus be exerted in the way of developing the character of the pupils." It was not denied that so far as pure instruction went specialists could do better, but that was entirely secondary to the other and higher aims of the school.

The large attendance on secondary schools in Germany furnishes, perhaps, the best proof that can be given of the interest taken by the Germans in higher education. From recent statistics it appears that fully seven per cent. of the pupils enrolled in German schools are attending secondary schools or schools in advance of the elementary schools. In Ontario the proportion is about five per cent., although it must be said that the standard for admission to a secondary school in Germany is not as high as that prescribed in the Province of Ontario. In Germany when a pupil completes his ninth year, that is to say, when he has finished the course of study prescribed for pupils of that age, he is admitted to a secondary school, the German system of instruction and inspection being so searching and so complete as practically to render unnecessary an entrance examination to a secondary school.

CHAPTER IX.

NORMAL SCHOOLS.

Number of Schools—Qualifications for Admission—Course of Study—Criticism Lessons—Examinations—Practical Tests—Normal School for Women—Examination of Teachers in High Schools.

There are in the entire empire about two hundred Normal Schools, more than half of which are in Prussia. Most of these institutions are supported by the state, some by cities, and some by private individuals. The schools for males and the schools for females are separate; a division more or less marked is made also on the basis of religion. For example, in Prussia, seventy-two schools are reported as Evangelical, thirty-seven Catholic, and five as placing religious beliefs on an equality (*paritat*).

As a rule these schools are not large, numbering in most cases not more than one hundred pupils. The classes are correspondingly small, each class having rarely more than forty pupils. In 1888 there were but five of the one hundred and fifteen Normal Schools of Prussia, which had upwards of one hundred pupils, and but one that had less than fifty pupils.

The number of teachers required for each Normal School in Prussia is seven; one principal, one head assistant and five other assistant teachers. In the year 1888 the average number of pupils to a teacher was about 12. The number of teachers above cited does not include the critic teachers, of whom there are two or more in every practice school.

The examination for admission to the Normal School is oral and written, embracing all subjects required to be taught in the elementary schools. The written work includes a theme upon a given subject and brief tests in the various studies. The oral examination is conducted by members of the faculty, each teacher generally examining in the subject which he teaches.

In Prussia candidates for entrance to a Normal School for males may not be under seventeen years of age, and not more than twenty-four. They must present certificates as to their physical condition and moral character, and must present a satisfactory guarantee that the father or guardian is able to pay their living expenses during the course. They pledge themselves to serve as teachers in the kingdom at least three years, under the penalty of forfeiting the cost of instruction and board. The syllabus of entrance requirements shows that no time of the Normal School course is expected to be given to teaching the subject matter of the elementary schools; or, if such matter is taught, it is mainly for discipline, and for the purpose of enabling the students to know the subjects from the teacher's standpoint.

The course of studies for the Normal School proper in Prussia, extends over three years, and includes: Pedagogics, Religion, German, History, Arithmetic, Geometry, Physics, Geography, Drawing, Writing, Gymnastics, Music (instrumental and vocal), Foreign Language (elective).

In Music, every student of the Normal School is required to learn to play upon some musical instrument, generally, in men's schools, upon the violin. Regular instruction, with several hours of practice weekly throughout the course, gives the students such facility in playing the violin or piano as to enable them to teach music well when they become teachers.

Tuition is free to all students who intend to teach. In boarding schools the expense of living is very small—in many cases less than eighty dollars a year. Assistance is given by the Government to indigent pupils, amounting in some cases to the entire cost of living.

Some of the Normal Schools have connected with them two practice schools for observation and practice, one ungraded and the other graded into four or more classes. The amount of observation and practice in the German Normal Schools is much greater than that required of Normal School students in Ontario, although in other respects there is little difference in the course of study.

The general practice in German Normal Schools is to devote the first year and a half to the study of Psychology or Pedagogics, as it is called, and to the general theory of instruction. During the last three months of the second year, model lessons are taught by the Master of Methods, in the presence of the class, for which each student is supposed to make a written preparation. On the first occasion on which the model lesson is given by the Master of Methods, much time is spent:—

(*a*) On discussion as to the best treatment of the subject given for a trial lesson.

(*b*) On Discussion of the written preparations which have been made for the lesson.

(c) The trial lesson itself, which is held in the Practice School.

(d) Criticism of the trial lesson which has been given.

In these discussions and criticisms the students are expected to take a part. The student is then prepared for work in the Practice School. The practice is to assign to a student the entire management of a class for a particular period. For the subjects which they are going to teach they are expected to make a careful and detailed preparation in writing. In order to assist them in making such preparation as will be most useful, lectures are given weekly as to the best methods of preparing lessons, and although these lectures may not apply specially to any particular subject, they are found helpful to the student by supplying him with hints as to methods and to sources of information. While engaged in the Practice School he is under the supervision of the Master of Methods or some other member of the staff, the other students present make notes in writing for future reference at the Criticism meeting. These notes refer to the number of questions put, the answers given to them, the personal peculiarities and mannerisms of expression of the student-teacher, the attitude of the class, etc.

Some days after these trial lessons have been given, a criticism meeting takes place in the class-room. At this meeting are read and discussed the criticisms of the students who were present while the practice lesson was taught, the reply of the students who taught the practice lesson, the criticism of the Master of Methods, followed by some observations from the Director.

The plan of discussion is as follows:

(1) Was the lesson held under the requisite conditions of quiet, temperature, light, etc. ?

(2) Was the bearing (action) of the teacher good ?

(3) Language of the teacher (intonation, rhythm, force, tone).

(4) Were the questions properly put and distributed ?

(5) Did the teacher or the pupils speak most ? "Self-activity" of pupils.

(6) How did the teacher treat the answers of the pupils ?

(7) Did he make proper use of the teaching apparatus ?

(8) Had he prepared himself sufficiently ?

(9) What as to his method (objective or subjective) ?

(10) Did he know how to maintain discipline ?

(11) Did he attain the object in view ?

As a rule these "criticisms" are very searching and thorough, and besides directing the student with respect to matters which have escaped his attention, they are exceedingly valuable in preventing the student from faulty methods in teaching and from mannerisms which might discredit his professional standing.

The final examination of the Training School is conducted by a commission composed of the commissary, of the Government Inspector in whose district the school is situated, the Director of the school and his staff; the School Inspectors for the district may also attend. The examination is both written and oral; the written examination consists of:

(1) An essay on the theory of education and instruction, or on some subject connected with the German language or literature.

(2) Notes for a lesson on some scripture subject.

(3) A paper to test the non-professional attainments of students in their course of study.

If the written examination is satisfactory the oral examination may be dispensed with. Then follows the practical part of the examination, which consists of a trial lesson in one of the obligatory subjects, for teaching which a candidate is allowed two days for preparation. A scheme of the lesson in writing must be handed in. Candidates who fail in German, Scripture or Arithmetic, or in more than three of the other subjects are disqualified. In the case of those who pass, their certificate shows their standing in each subject.

Although there is no fixed age which the candidate must reach before obtaining a certificate, yet it is seldom that a young man enters upon the profession in Germany under twenty years.

The Final Teachers' Examination.—Not earlier than two years after their first examination, teachers must pass the final examination. They are then assured of pay for life, even should the schools where they are employed cease to exist.

The committee is the same as that for the first examination.

Candidates must submit:

(1) A certificate from the School Commissioner.

(2) An essay, stating authorities used, and certifying that they have received no assistance from other sources.

(3) A drawing, with a certificate that the candidate has received no assistance in preparing the same.

(4) A specimen of penmanship under the same conditions.

These four particulars determine the admission or non-admission of candidates to the examination.

Candidates may endeavor to raise the standing attained at the first teachers' examination, or he may try the voluntary subjects.

The written test consists of a theme on some subject connected with school management, a theme relating to religious instruction, and one touching instruction in one of the other common school branches. Jewish candidates substitute another subject in place of religious instruction. This work is chosen by the chairman of the Examining Committee upon recommendation of the Normal School Faculty for the district in which the examination is held. The work must be done in the presence of a member of the committee.

The practical test consists of a class exercise, the subject for which is announced the day before.

The oral test covers the history of education, principles of education, school management and methods of teaching. At the discretion of the committee, questions may be asked touching positive knowledge of subject matter. Candidates are marked " very good," " good," " sufficient," " not sufficient," as the case may be.

Candidates who fail to attain the mark " sufficient " in the class exercise, are rejected. Results in other respects are determined as at the first examination.

Successful candidates receive certificates showing the standing attained in each subject. The committee then licenses the candidates to teach permanently.

Candidates failing to attain a higher standing than at the first examination in the subjects in which they have been re-examined, are, nevertheless, permanently licensed, if other work has been satisfactory.

Candidates who received the standing "good" in Religion, Language, Arithmetic, Geography, History and Natural History (or instead of the last three a foreign language), at the first examination or the final examination, and who, at the final examination received the same mark in all subjects, are legally qualified to teach in the lower classes of middle schools, and higher schools for girls.

Teachers are qualified to serve as assistants and to give private instructions within the standard of an Elementary School. They may be assigned as assistants at the head of a preparatory Training School, and in such cases would be under the immediate supervision of their principal in and out of school. When the probationary period has expired, whether it be two or more years, a provisional teacher is annually called upon by the school authorities to present himself for the second examination. If he fails to pass this examination within the time prescribed, which, in Prussia, is six years after passing the Normal School examination, he is disqualified for further service. The final examination consists of a written examination and a practical test corresponding in its main features to the final examination of the Normal School.

Normal Schools for Women.—The employment of women as teachers in Germany has not yet met with the same favor as in England or Canada. Out of 64,750 regular teachers employed in the Public Elementary Schools, 6,849 were females. Where they are employed it is generally in the lowest primary divisions of graded schools. It is seldom they are found in ungraded schools. There are nine State Normal Schools for training women to become school teachers in Prussia, and three Training Schools for Governesses. These institutions are conducted on the residential principle, the tuition and living expenses at the Training School for Teachers amounting to sixty dollars annually, with extras amounting to sixteen and eighteen dollars. Training Schools for Governesses cost annually from $100 to $110. Candidates for admission to a Normal School for Women must have the same qualifications, except in Music, as those for admission to other Normal Schools. In addition they must have taken a course in industrial training for girls. They must not be under seventeen years of age, nor over twenty-four. The course covers two years for teachers and three years for governesses. At the close of the course, examinations are held. Candidates for teachers' certificates, if successful, receive a license to teach in the Elementary School. Governesses receive a license to teach in a private school as governesses, or in middle or higher schools for girls. The final examination is conducted after the same method as in the case of males, and is both theoretical and practical.

Examination of Teachers in the Higher Schools.— Other and more severe examinations are given to candidates for the position of teacher in the middle and higher grades of middle schools and higher schools for girls, and also for the principalship of Elementary Schools.

Candidates for the position of teacher in High Schools (Gymnasia, Realgymnasia, and Oberrealschulen, and Hoheren Bergerschulen), are examined by "scientific examination commissions," consisting of seven members, one for each of the principal subjects in which the candidates are examined.

Candidates are required to have graduated from a Gymnasium or Realgymnasium, and to have studied three years in a University. The examination is written and oral. Besides a brief biography, written in Latin, or in French or English, candidates have two or three essays to write upon given subjects, being allowed six weeks' time for each essay. In certain cases the dissertation written to secure the doctor's degree in the University is received in lieu of the essays above mentioned. Several oral and written tests are given in the subjects selected by the candidates as main subjects, while in other branches, notably, Philosophy, Pedagogics, German Language and Literature, and Religion, candidates are obliged to prove their efficiency. Having received a certificate—conditional or unconditional—indicating his fitness for one or another position, the candidate is obliged to spend a certain period of time in Gymnasium or a Realgymnasium under the direction of the principal, before he can receive a permanent appointment. Formerly the time spent in practice was one year, being called a trial year (Probejahr). In 1882 the trial period was extended to two years, after which candidates pass another examination, in which they show that their time has been profitably spent in the observation and practice of good methods of teaching. In 1889 it was decreed that seven pedagogical seminaries should be established in every province, to be connected with the Gymnasium. A candidate for the position of teacher in a gymnasium is expected to spend a year in the seminary under the direction of a Gymnasium Director. During this trial year of teaching he is paid a small amount by the Government.

CHAPTER X.

MISCELLANEOUS.

Organization of Schools — Inspections—Mode of Appointing Teachers—Pensions—School Houses—School Terms—Text-books—Teachers' Conferences—Grants to Education—General Review.

The school system of Germany, as already stated, like the school system of Canada and the United States, is under the direct administration of Provincial School Boards which have charge of the higher schools of the Province.

The District Governments have charge of the people's schools and of the greater part of the girls' high schools and all private institutions.

Some of the higher schools are supported wholly by the General Government, some by both General and Local Governments together, and some by Local Governments and private persons and societies. There is a local board which is charged mainly with the local administration of the schools, such as attending to repairs of buildings, fixing school fees, and, in certain cases, nominating teachers. For private and municipal schools the local school authorities nominate teachers, but confirmation is always left to the Provincial or district authorities.

For purposes of inspection the country is divided into districts. Inspectors are selected for distinguished service as teachers and are charged with duties somewhat similar to our school inspectors in Ontario. Besides visiting the ordinary schools, the Inspector is required to visit private schools, to fill temporarily vacancies in the teaching staff and to hold at least once a year a conference with all the teachers of the district. In Prussia he has to pass judgment upon plans of school buildings and alterations.

Where the country districts are large, local inspectors are appointed who are generally clergymen and who serve without pay. Their duties are mainly supervisory.

The examinations conducted by the Inspectors are very searching and are beyond question conclusive tests of the efficiency of the schools so far as the work of teachers and pupils is concerned.

Where the schools are large, say ten to twelve teachers, the Principal of the school seldom teaches more than twelve hours a week, i.e., about $2\frac{1}{2}$ hours per day. The object of this is to permit him to look after the administration of the schools and to oversee the work of his assistants.

The method of appointing teachers varies in different parts of the Empire. In some Provinces appointments are made by the Government, i.e., by Boards representing the Government; nominations for private and municipal schools are made by the local boards; these nominations are always confined to persons who have passed the requisite examinations. In Prussia teachers are permitted to leave their schools only at the close of a term and must give three months' notice of their intention to leave unless excused by the school board from such notice·

Certain appointments of elementary teachers are made for three years, and within that time the teachers so appointed are not permitted to resign. To prevent a too frequent change of teachers the practice in some graded schools is to have the teacher follow his class as it is promoted from grade to grade.

The average yearly salary of all elementary teachers of Prussia, in 1886, counting what is allowed some teachers for a dwelling, was $318.75. Many teachers, however, receive extra compensation for services as choir masters and organists. The average salary in rural districts is $281. Although these salaries appear to be small, the German teacher has compensating advantages as compared with the teacher of Ontario. In the case of disability, he receives a pension from the Government and his family certain assistance on his death. In Berlin, after ten years' service, the teacher's pension, if he be disabled, amounts to one-quarter of the salary of the last year. After forty years' service the pension amounts to three-quarters of the last year's salary. In several of the Provinces, the allowances for pensions is even more liberal. In Prussia and Saxony, teachers are not required to contribute to the pension fund as the state and separate municipalities assume the whole charge for pensions. In other parts of Germany the teachers are required to contribute a certain percentage of their salaries to the pension fund. On the death of a teacher a percentage of his pension goes to his wife and children.

Teachers are excused from paying taxes, and they have but six weeks' military service, instead of a service of one year or three years, as is required of other able-bodied male citizens.

One reason why the teachers are contented with the salaries that are paid them is, that when once appointed, they hold their office practically during life, or good behavior. Rarely is a teacher dismissed from service, and then only after repeated complaints by the Superintendent and principal. The fear that teachers if given a life tenure, would neglect their work, is not sustained by experience in Germany.

German schoolhouses are generally of a very plain character, although in the larger cities they are becoming more modern in their equipment and more artistic in design. The seats and desks would not be considered very suitable or convenient in Ontario, and the blackboard facilities are far too meagre to suit the necessities of the Ontario teacher. By law a portrait of the Emperor is required to be hung in every schoolroom. Each teacher has his own room, as in Ontario, and generally the same class from day to day. Special teachers, i.e., teachers who take one or two subjects, go from room to room as may be prescribed in the time table.

The school term is from forty-two to forty-five weeks in the year with vacations at Easter, Midsummer, Whitsuntide, and Christmas. The school sessions in summer are from seven to eleven a. m.; in winter, from eight to twelve a. m.; and in the afternoon from two to four. In rural districts the schools sometimes close at eleven o'clock to give children an opportunity of assisting their parents on the farm and in the garden.

Registers for marking the attendance of children are used as in Ontario. Promotions, as a rule, are made by the Principal without any formal written examination.

The Principal is guided in his judgment by the teacher's opinion of the pupils' merits. The leaving examinations which occurs at the close of the course in the higher schools are very difficult and comprehensive. In the Gymnasium and Realschule they determine the student's fitness for the University and Technological School, and correspond with our Matriculation Examinations. The school age is from six to fifteen.

The German text-book, except in reading, is usually a mere outline of the subject. Teachers, as a rule, make no use of a text-book except by way of reference in the school room. It would take many text-books to contain the information which he is expected to give on every subject on the curriculum. The method of selecting text-books varies in the different Provinces. In some institutions their selection is in the hands of the local district board, in other cases the Minister of Instruction has the sole power of authorizing text-books. The Provincial School Board may, in some cases, permit the introduction of a new text-book on the recommendation of the principal and his associate teachers, such recommendation being accompanied by a statement of reasons for the use of the new book. Where pupils are unable to furnish their own text-books they are supplied by the Government. Many schools are well supplied with books for the use of teachers on the methods of teaching the various subjects, as well as upon the subject matter to be taught. Nearly every German school is well supplied with apparatus for illustrating Chemistry, Physics and Mathematics as well as with charts for instruction in Natural History and Philosophy.

In the Elementary Schools of Prussia the following appliances are, by law, required to be provided :

A copy of every text-book used in school ; a globe ; a wall map of the home Province ; a wall map of Germany ; a wall map of Palestine ; charts for instruction in Natural History and Philosophy ; large alphabets of wood or of pasteboard ; a violin ; a rule and a pair of compasses ; a numeral frame ; models for teaching Geometry ; two blackboards; for Protestant schools, a Bible and a copy of the song book used in the district.

As a means of keeping up a high professional standard among teachers, and of exercising a strong influence upon public opinion and legislation in relation to education, there are maintained throughout the Empire a great number of associations of teachers. These exist in great variety, representing all kinds and grades of teachers, from the little organized circle of village teachers to the National Union, now numbering nearly 40,000 members. It is estimated that there are now upwards of 60,000 active paying members of the various associations.

In some parts of Germany the time given to home study for pupils of the Elementary Schools is limited by law or decree as follows :—For pupils of the lower grade, one hour ; of the middle grades, one hour and one half ; of the upper grades, two hours.

No limit appears to be placed upon the amount of time devoted to study in High Schools. The present Emperor, in a speech before a recent conference for school reform, declared that the time given for home study by the pupils of class *prima* of the Gymnasium was from five and one-half to seven hours a day. This is probably an extravagant statement. It is safe to say, however, that the pupils of all grades in Germany study more out of school than do pupils of the same grade and age in Ontario. This disparity may be due in part to the fact that no time is allowed for study in school, every portion of the school day being given to recitations.

Pupils of all ages seem to be subject to the control of school authorities to a far greater extent than in Ontario Pupils of High Schools in Prussia are forbidden to absent themselves from the city or town over night, to attend theatres and balls, or receive private lessons, without permission from the teacher or director. They are forbidden to frequent saloons and taverns, and may not attend certain public performances, except in company with their parents or guardians. Alcoholic liquor or beer cannot be sold to children of school age.

In many parts of Germany no one, not even a parent or friend of the pupils, is allowed to visit the school at any time, without permission from the constituted authorities. To visit the High Schools one must get written permission from the Minister of Instruction or Provincial School Board.

The grants to education in 1888 were $50,192,857, divided as follows:

Universities	$ 3,769,405
High Schools and Seminaries	6,940,119
Elementary instruction	37,357,857
Trade Schools	2,125,476

Of this sum the state contributed 31 per cent., the district 46 per cent., other revenues and funds 22 per cent. The cost per head of public education in Prussia was, in 1888, 1.77 of the total population.

General Review.—A brief summary of the principal features of the German schools may be helpful in determining their chief characteristics:

(1) Education is compulsory from six to fourteen years of age; in Ontario, from eight to fourteen years of age.

(2) Schools open in summer at seven o'clock in the morning, in winter at eight o'clock; in Ontario they open at nine o'clock. The afternoon school term in Germany is two hours; in Ontario in Elementary Schools it is usually three hours The noon vacation in Germany is from twelve to two in Elementary Schools; in Ontario it is usually from twelve to one.

(3) Grammar Schools are still furnished with double desks or with forms where four or five pupils sit together; in Ontario forms have been abolished and the practice is in favor of a desk for each pupil.

(4) German schools are badly supplied with blackboards; Ontario schools, as a rule, are well supplied.

(5) The maps and apparatus of German schools are usually superior to those of the schools of Ontario.

(6) In point of architecture and attractiveness externally, German Elementary School buildings are inferior to those of Ontario.

(7) The work of the primary classes in Germany, although the methods are scientific and progressive, as a rule, is more taxing and severe than the corresponding work in Ontario schools.

(8) Discipline is more rigid and the school life of the German pupil seems to be less pleasant and happy than school life in Ontario.

Among the subjects receiving greater attention in German schools than in Ontario may be mentioned the following:

(1) Music, is taught in every grade and with splendid results.

(2) Gymnastics receive greater attention.

(3) Natural History, Observation Lessons, the study of common objects and simple instruction in Elementary Science have a very prominent place in the curriculum of studies.

(4) Religion particularly, so far as it refers to the historical parts of the Bible.

(5) History, in its relation to the Empire and so far as it is calculated to develop a patriotic spirit and a love of the Fatherland.

(6) Geography, Arithmetic and Reading are well taught but they cannot be said to receive relatively the same attention or to be deemed of equal importance educationally as the other subjects.

Teachers.—All the German teachers both in Elementary and Secondary Schools are professionally trained.

(2) Ninety per cent. of the school room instruction is given without the use of a text-book.

(3) The teacher's manner is less cheerful and sympathetic and his tone of voice generally more dictatorial.

(4) He is the ideal of thoroughness and accuracy.

(5) His tenure of office is more permanent than that of the teacher of Ontario.

(6) He is regarded by the government as a member of the Civil Service.

(7) He draws a pension on retirement.

(8) His family are provided for by the State.

(9) His social position is high.

Only 10,600 women teachers, or $14\frac{1}{4}$ per cent. of all the teaching force of the kingdom were employed in 1887 in the German Elementary, Middle and Secondary Schools.

Training Schools.—The professional training is combined with the Academic Course. Psychology and the History of Education form an important part of the curriculum. The course extends over three years at least. Practical teaching is not permitted until after a careful study of methods. The final examination tests the student in both the theory and practice of teaching. The full standing of the teacher is not obtained until after at least two years' experience as a provisional teacher. Professional training is required in every class of schools from Private Schools up to the Gymnasium.

CHAPTER XI.

GENERAL CONCLUSIONS.

Central Administration—Minister of Education—Local Administration—Managers and Boards of Trustees—Elections—Teachers—Training Schools—Inspection—Text-Books—Place of Secondary Schools in English and German Systems of Education.

In England and Prussia as well as in nearly all the States of Germany the Department of Education is directed either by a Minister of Education or by an officer with all the power of a Minister. Under the English system, the Vice-President of the Privy Council, who holds a seat in the House of Commons, is responsible for the administration of the Education Department.

Occasional demands are made through the public press and by teachers' meetings for the appointment of a Minister of Education, but so far these demands appear not to have been seriously entertained by either political party. The House of Commons, under the Education Act, retains the right to approve or disapprove of all the regulations of the Education Department affecting the distribution of the school grants and the qualifications of teachers, leaving the Department, through its officers and

Inspectors for to administer the law in harmony with the various statutes in that behalf. These large powers the Department appears to have exercised with good judgment and in the public interest. The brevity with which the educational estimates are discussed in Parliament, shows the confidence which prevails in the administration of educational affairs by the Department.

With regard to the local administration of schools both in England and Germany the Boards of Managers or as we would call them in Ontario, Trustees, are invested only with limited powers :

(1) The character of the school buildings to be erected, the nature of the school site, the accommodation for pupils as to air, space, lighting and ventilation, desks and equipment are defined by the educational authorities in each case. The rules of the Department in England with respect to buildings are very strict. The code provides that " All new school premises and enlargements must conform generally to the rules contained in Schedule 7 (see Appendix E) and the plans must be approved by the Department before such new premises and enlargements are passed."

In this respect the supervision of the Department is more rigid than in the Province of Ontario. Although with us the grant may be withheld for insufficient accommodation still in the case of Public Schools the approval of the plans of the building by the Department prior to their erection is not required. In the case of High Schools it is required that the plans should be submitted for approval as trustees were often disappointed after having spent a large sum of money, in finding their schools rated second or third class where the same expenditure would have given them a high rating had greater attention been paid to details.

In England any ratepayer irrespective of sex may vote for or may be elected trustee. The system of election under the London School Board follows what is called the cumulative principle. The city is divided into districts and every ratepayer in the district has as many votes as there are trustees to be elected. These votes he may poll in favor of one candidate or as many candidates as he approves not exceeding the number to be elected. Under this system it is considered that the most capable men for the office of school trustee can be obtained. I have no doubt that the application of such a system to the large cities of the Province of Ontario would be of advantage. While on the whole our city systems have been admirably administered it sometimes happens that men of superior fitness are passed over because others anxious for distinction make their elections a personal matter and press themselves upon the attention of the ratepayers. Compared generally, however, with the system of local management which prevails in Ontario either as to elasticity, enterprise or progressiveness, we have little to learn from England or from Germany.

Teachers.—As in Ontario, so in England and Germany, the licensing of teachers is controlled by the Education Department. The underlying principle seems to be that so long as the state holds itself responsible for the education of the people it must see, not only that the appliances for that purpose are adequate but that those to whom the work of instruction is entrusted are properly qualified. Acting on that principle the State prescribes the standard for the different grades of teachers, determines the examinations they shall pass, conducts the examinations by officers of its own appointment, determines the age at which they shall be admitted to the profession and pronounces at all times upon their fitness, both morally and intellectually, for continuing in the profession. The methods adopted for determining the qualifications of teachers in England and Germany are in many respects similar to those now prevailing in Ontario.

In England teachers are classified as :

(*a*) Candidates on probation.

(*b*) Pupil teachers.

(*c*) Assistant teachers.

(*d*) Provisionally certificated teachers.

(*e*) Certificated teachers.

(*f*) Additional female teachers approved by the Inspector.

(*g*) Night school teachers.

In Germany the gradation is mainly based upon experience.

The Education Department prescribes the examination which teachers shall pass and the mode of conducting them and as in Ontario now, such examinations are in the hands of experts.

So far however, the teaching profession has much less to do with maintaining its own standards in England than it has in Canada as the examination papers of all candidates from the " Pupil teacher " up are read by the Inspectors or under his immediate supervision instead of by experienced members of the profession as in Ontario. In the Training Colleges, the Inspector of Training Colleges and the faculty have the full right to pass or pluck all teachers in training

With regard to the attainments, both educationally and professionally, of English and German teachers it may be said that they are in no sense inferior to those of the teachers of Ontario. Their course of instruction has equally as wide a range and the examination papers are quite as searching. My observation too, of their methods in the school room, their power of maintaining discipline and the clearness and enthusiasm with which they conduct their schools make it quite apparent that in all the qualities which constitute good teaching the great majority of them would rank high in this Province.

Training Schools.—The Training Schools of England are directly under the control of the Department as in Ontario and are subject to periodical inspection. I have already intimated that the majority of them are residential, Day Schools, as they are called, for the training of teachers being of recent origin. The Training Colleges unlike our Normal Schools, are however, under a Board of Managers who have the same powers generally with respect to them as Managers exercise over Elementary Schools. The State aids the Managers in the erection or enlargement of their buildings and as shown elsewhere gives substantial aid for maintenance also. The authority of the Department, however, is direct and absolute with regard to the curriculum of studies, inspection and examinations.

Inspection.—In England and Germany the Inspectors are appointed by the Education Department and are paid their salaries and travelling expenses out of the appropriation voted for that purpose. Inspectors in English schools are nearly all graduates of one of the large Universities; experience as a teacher in an Elementary School has not hitherto been required as a perequisite for such an appointment although the tendency of public opinion will no doubt influence the Department in making appointments in future with this qualification in view In Germany, professional experience is deemed essential. The mode of inspection in both countries is almost identical with that prevailing here. The Inspector is supposed to examine the pupils in every subject in the school curriculum as well as to observe one or two recitations conducted by the teacher himself. It is his duty to report upon the attendance of the school, the cleanliness of the school room and of the pupils, the efficiency of the teacher, and generally upon such matters as would indicate whether the school was properly and efficiently conducted. The instructions given by the Department to an Inspector, already set forth, sufficiently show the character of his work. The recognition which the Department has given the profession in connection with this important service in Ontario is in striking contrast with the practice still prevailing in England.

Text-Books.—In the choice of Text-Books both in England and Germany teachers are under little or no restraint. Whether the Text-Books are supplied by the Board as in London and in all other schools under the Act of 1891, this liberty is of comparatively little consequence to the ratepayer. Where pupils purchase their own Text-Books as in Ontario with the exception of Toronto, the restrictions which prevail here and with more or less stringency in nearly all the cities of the American Union are absolutely necessary and an essential part of our School system. As to the quality of the Text-Books supplied we need have no fear of comparison with England or Germany. In binding, typography and illustrations our text books are not inferior; as to grading and arrangement and selection of material I believe ours are superior. In England the Text-Book occupies in the hands of the teacher about the same place as it does in Ontario; in Germany the teacher is expected to be all but independent of the Text-Book and in that respect the German teacher is in advance both of Ontario and England.

Secondary Schools.—What may be called the English system of education begins and ends with Elementary Schools. Her Secondary Schools, if such they may be called, have no connection with the Elementary Schools below, or the Universities above, them. The Education Department has no control over the accommodation required for pupils, over their courses of study or over the qualifications of their teachers. Any inspection to which they are submitted is purely voluntary on the part of masters. They receive no State aid and acknowledge no responsibility to any authority except that of their own managers. As to the efficiency of many of them there can be no question although it is quite certain that the greater number would not long survive the competition of a well conducted system of Secondary schools such as we have in Ontario. The German Secondary Schools as already explained constitute an integral part of the School system of the State or Province to which they belong. Pupils who have passed through certain grades of the Volkschulen proceed as a matter of course to a Secondary School according to the course of study which they intend afterwards to pursue. The leaving examination which they pass on completing their course of study at such Elementary School admits them to the University without further examination. The supervision over Secondary education in Germany is quite as strict as in the case of Elementary Schools and the training and qualification of teachers provides adequate guarantees for their efficiency. The School of Pedagogy recently established in Ontario corresponds with the training given in the German Seminar for Secondary teachers.

APPENDIX A.

COURSE OF STUDY IN ENGLISH ELEMENTARY SCHOOLS.

The following limit table prescribed by the Education Department will show the course of study in each standard; one standard being considered the limit of the pupil's progress for each year :—

NOTE—The seven standards constitute a course about equal to the five forms in the Public Schools of Ontario.

READING.

Standard I.—To read a short passage from a book not confined to words of one syllable.

Standard II.—To read a short passage from an elementary reading book.

Standard III.—To read a passage from a reading book.

Standard IV.—To read a passage from a reading book, or history of England.

Standard V.—To read a passage from some standard author, a reading book, or a history of England.

Standard VI.—To read a passage from one of Shakespeare's historical plays, or from other standard authors, or from a history of England.

Standard VII.—To read a passage from Shakespeare or Milton, or from some other standard author, or from a history of England.

Writing.

Standard I.—Copy in manuscript characters a line of print, commencing with a capital letter. Copy books (large of half text hand) to be shown.

Standard II.—A passage of not more than six lines, from the same book, slowly read once, and then dictated word by word. Copy books (large and half text hand) to be shown.

Standard III.—Six lines from one of the reading books of the Standard, slowly read once, and then dictated. Copy books (capitals and figures, large and small hand) to be shown.

Standard IV.—Eight lines of poetry or prose, slowly read once, and then dictated. Copy books to be shown.

Standard V.—Writing from memory the substance of a short story read out twice; spelling, handwriting, and correct expression to be considered. Copy books to be shown.

Standard VI.—A short theme or letter on an easy subject; spelling, handwriting and composition to be considered. Copy books to be shown.

Standard VII.—A theme or letter. Composition, spelling and handwriting to be considered. Note books and exercise books to be shown.

Arithmetic.

Standard I.—Notation and Numeration up to 1,000. Simple addition and subtraction of numbers of not more than three figures. In addition not more than five lines to be given. The Multiplication table to 6 times 12.

Standard II.—Notation and Numeration up to 100,000. The four simple rules to short division. The Multiplication table and the Pence table to 12s.

Standard III.—The former rules, with long division. Addition and subtraction of money.

IV.—Compound rules (money) and reduction of common weights and measures.

Standard V.—Practice, bills of parcels, and single rule of three by the method of unity. Addition and subtraction of proper fractions, with denominators not exceeding 12.

Standard VI.—Fractions, vulgar and decimal; simple proportion and simple interest. (Questions involving recurring decimals will not be put to girls)

Standard VII.—Averages, percentages and stocks.

Short exercises in Mental Arithmetic may be given in the examination of II standards. These should not involve large numbers, should from the first deal with concrete as well as abstract quantities, and should be preparatory to the work of the next higher standard.

In Welsh Districts.—Bi-lingual reading books and copy books may be used, and the instruction generally may be bi-lingual.

Translation into English of an easy piece of Welsh written on the blackboard, or of a story read twice, shall, if the Managers so desire, be substituted for composition.

In the Arithmetic set to Standards I-IV inclusive, the problems should be in both English and Welsh.

Historical reading books should relate to the history of England and Wales.

English.

Standard I.—Pointing out nouns.

Standard II.—Pointing out nouns and verbs.

Standard III.—Pointing out nouns, verbs, adjectives, adverbs, and personal pronouns, and forming simple sentence containing them.

Standard IV.—Parsing easy sentences, and showing by examples the use of each of the parts of speech.

Standard V.—Parsing and Analysis of simple sentences. The method of forming English nouns, adjectives and verbs from each other.

Standard VI.—Parsing and analysis of a short complex sentence. The meaning and use of the most common Latin prefixes in the formation of English words.

Standard VII.—Analysis of sentences. The most common prefixes and terminations generally.

Geography.

Standard I.—A plan of the school and playground. The four cardinal points. The meaning and use of a map.

Standard II.—The size and shape of the world. Geographical terms simply explained, and illustrated by reference to the map of England. Physical geography of hills and rivers.

Standard III.—Physical and political geography of England, with special knowledge of the district in which the school is situated.

Standard IV.—Physical and political geography of the British Isles, and of British North America and Australasia, with knowledge of their productions.

Standard V.—Geography of Europe, physical and political. Latitude and Longitude. Day and Night. The Seasons.

Standard VI.—The British colonies and dependencies. Interchange of productions. Circumstances which determine climate.

Standard VII.—The United States. Tides and chief ocean currents.

ELEMENTARY SCIENCE.

Standard I.—Thirty days on common subjects, *e. g.*, a postage stamp; the post; money; a lead pencil; a railway train; foods and clothing materials, as bread, milk, cotton, wool; minerals; natural phenomena, as gold, coal, the day, the year.

Standard II.—Thirty lessons on common objects, such as animals, plants, and substances employed in ordinary life, *e. g.*, horse, sparrow, roots, stems, buds, leaves, candles, soap, cork, paper.

Standard III.—Simple principles of classification of plants and animals. Substances used in the arts and manufactures. Phenomena of the earth and atmosphere.

Standard IV.—A more advanced knowledge of special groups of common objects, such as :—

(*a*) Animals, or plants, with particular reference to agriculture; or

(*b*) Substances employed in arts and manufactures; or

(*c*) Some simple kinds of physical and mechanical appliances, *e. g.*, the thermometer, barometer, lever pulley, wheel and axle, spirit level.

Standard V.—

(*a*) Animal or plant life; or

(*b*) The principles and processes involved in one of the chief industries of England; or

(*c*) The physical and mechanical principles involved in the construction of some common instruments, and of simple forms of industrial machinery.

Standard VI.—

(*a*) Animal and plant life; or

(*b*) The commonest elements, and their compounds; or

(*c*) The mechanical powers.

Standard VII.—

(*a*) Distribution of plants and animals, and of the races of mankind; or

(*b*) Properties of common gases; or

(*c*) Sound, or light, or heat, or electricity, with applications.

HISTORY.

Standard I & II—Simple stories relating to English History.

Standard III. Twelve stories from early English History, *e.g.* the Ancient Britons, the introduction of Christianity, Alfred the Great, Canute, Harold, The Norman Conquest.

Standard IV.—Twenty stories and biographies from 1066 to 1485, *e.g.*, Becket, Richard I. and the Crusades, John and Magna Charta, Montfort and the House of Commons, the Black Prince, Caxton.

Standard V.—The Tudor period, with biographies of leading persons, *e. g.*, the Protector Somerset, Queen Elizabeth, Shakespeare, Raleigh, Cecil, Drake, Mary Queen of Scots.

Standard VI.—The Stuart period, with special reference to the Civil War, and to the Constitution and functions of Parliament. Biographies of six leading persons.

Standard VII.—The Hanoverian period, with special reference to the acquisition and growth of the colonies and foreign possessions of Great Britain. Biographies of six eminent writers or statesmen.

In districts where Welsh is spoken the intelligence of the children examined in any elementary or class subjects shall, if the Managers so desire, be tested by requiring them to explain in Welsh the meaning of passages read, and bi-lingual books may be used for the purpose of instructing the scholars.

It should be observed with regard to these courses of study in Class Subjects, such as English, Geography, Science and History, that the Managers are at liberty to adopt any other division of these subjects, subject to the approval of the Inspector. Besides, these subjects themselves are optional.

NEEDLEWORK.

Below Standard I.—Needle drill; Position drill, Strips (18 inches by 2 inches) in simple hemming with coloured cotton, in the following order, viz.: 1. Black; 2. Red; 3. Blue. Knitting-pin drill. A strip knitted (15 inches by 3 inches) in cotton or wool.

Standard I.—1. Hemming, seaming, felling. Any garment or other useful article, showing these stitches, *e g.*, a child's pinafore, pillow-case, or pocket handkerchief.

2. Knitting. Two needles, plain, *e. g.*, a strip or a comforter.

Standard II.—1. The work of the previous standard with greater skill. Any garment or other useful article, as above.

2. Knitting. Two needles, plain and purled, *e. g.*, cuffs.

Standard III.—1 The work of the previous Standards, stitching on coarse material, pleating and sewing on strings. Garment: a pinafore, shift or apron. Herring-bone stitch. The stitch only on canvas or flannel. Darning, simple; on canvas.

2. Knitting: Four needles, plain and purled, *e. g.*, cuffs.

Standard IV.—1. The work of the previous Standards, gathering, setting-in, button-hole, sewing on button. Garment: a plain night-shirt, night-gown or petticoat, or any garment showing these stitches.

2. Darning: plain (as for this places) in stocking-web material.

3. Knitting: Four needles, a sock.

4. Herring-bone: a patch (at least three inches square) on coarse flannel.

5. Cutting out, in paper, an infant's shirt and a simple pinafore.

Standard V.—1. The work of the previous standards, and the running of a tuck. Garment as in Standard IV., to be cut out by the maker.

2. Knitting: Four needles, a sock or stocking, ribbed or plain.

3. Plain darning of a hole in stocking-web material.

4. Patching in calico.

5. Cutting out, in paper and in material, garments suitable for making up in Standard III.

6. Marking, simple, on canvas.

Standard VI.—1. The work of previous Standards. Garment: A baby's night-gown, or child's frock, or any garment showing the stitches of the previous Standards, to be cut out by the maker.

2. Darning, plain, on coarse linen.

3. Patching in print.

4. Knitting: Four needles, a stocking or sock.

5. Cutting out, in paper and in material, any under-garment for making up in Standard IV.

Standard VII.—1. The work of Standard VI., and whip-stitch and setting-on frill.

APPENDIX B

COURSE OF STUDY FOR PUPIL TEACHERS.

READING.

First Year.—To read with fluency, ease and just expression, and to repeat fifty lines of poetry.

In Welsh districts to read with fluency, ease and just expression in Welsh and English, and to repeat fifty lines of Welsh (or English) poetry.

Second Year.—To read as above, and to recite eighty lines of poetry, with knowledge of meanings and allusions

In Welsh districts to read as above, and to recite sixty lines of Welsh (or English) poetry, and to give the English (or Welsh) equivalents for words or short phrases in the piece selected.

Third Year.—To read as above, and to recite 100 lines of poetry, with knowledge of meanings and allusions.

In Welsh districts to read as above, and to recite eighty lines of poetry (half of which must be English) with translation of words and phrases.

Fourth Year.—To read as above, and to recite 100 lines of Shakespeare or Milton with clearness and force, and knowledge of meanings and allusions.

N.B.—The passages for repetition must be of a secular character, and taken from some standard English writer approved by Her Majesty's Inspector.

In Welsh districts to read as above, and to recite 100 lines (half of which must be in English) from standard authors with clearness and force, and knowledge of meanings and allusions.

English Grammar and Composition.

First Year.—Parsing and analysis of simple sentences, with knowledge of the ordinary terminations of English words. Writing from memory the substance of a passage of simple prose, read with ordinary quickness. Penmanship.

In Welsh districts parsing and analysis of simple sentences, with knowledge of the ordinary terminations of Welsh words. Writing in Welsh the substance of a short story read once. Penmanship.

Second Year.—Parsing and analysis of sentences, with knowledge of the chief Latin prefixes and terminations. Paraphrase of a short passage of poetry. Penmanship.

In Welsh districts parsing and analysis of sentences, with knowledge of the ordinary terminations of English words. Translation from Welsh into English of a short easy passage. Penmanship.

Third Year.—Parsing, analysis and paraphrase of complex sentences. Prefixes and affixes generally. Knowledge of the simple tests by which English words may be distinguished from those of foreign origin. Penmanship.

In Welsh districts parsing and analysis, with knowledge of Welsh and English prefixes and affixes generally. Translation from Welsh into English of a short passage. Penmanship.

Fourth Year.—Fuller knowledge of grammar and analysis, and of the common Latin roots of English words. Outline of the history of the language and literature. Penmanship.

In Welsh districts Welsh and English grammar Knowledge of the chief Latin roots of English words, with their cognates in Welsh. Penmanship.

Instead of this subject Latin may be taken in four stages, arranged as follows :—

LATIN.

First Year.—Grammar to the end of regular verbs with simple exercises in translation. Irregular verbs and first rules of Syntax. Knowledge of Delectus or other first Latin reading book. Translation of simple sentences of English (three or four words) into Latin.

Second Year.—The Latin Grammar. Cæsar, De Bello Gallico, Book I. Somewhat longer sentences to be translated from English into Latin.

Third Year.—Grammar. Composition of short Latin sentences. Cæsar, De Bello Gallico, Book II.

Fourth Year.—Grammar. More advanced composition. Virgil, Æneid, Book I. Pupil teachers taking this course instead of English grammar and composition in the Queen's Scholarship examination cannot also take Latin as a language

ARITHMETIC AND MATHEMATICS.—BOYS.

First Year.—Vulgar and decimal fractions, with their applications.

Second Year.—Proportion, with its applications to interest, averages, percentages and stocks. Euclid, Book I., to Prop. XXVI., with simple deductions.

Third Year.—Arithmetic generally, including the extraction of the square root. Euclid, Book I., with simple deductions. Mensuration of triangles and parrelograms. Algebra to simple equations (inclusive).*

Fourth Year.—Arithmetic, Euclid, Book II., with simple deductions. Mensuration of plane surfaces. Algebra to quadratic equations (inclusive).†

ARITHMETIC AND MENSURATION.—GIRLS.

First Year.—Practice, tradesmen's and household accounts. Measures and multiples, with addition and substraction of vulgar fractions.

Second Year.—Vulgar fractions, with their applications to money, weights and measures. Reduction of vulgar fractions to decimals.

Third Year.—Decimals and simple proportion.

Fourth Year.—Application of fractions and proportion to interest, discount, percentages, averages and stocks.

On the occasion of Her Majesty's Inspector's visit to the school, female pupil teachers must be prepared to afford evidence of their skill in teaching needle work, by a lesson given in his presence in their first year to the Third Standard, advancing a standard in each successive year of their engagement.

---

* Addition, substraction, multiplication, division, Greatest Common Measure, Least Common Multiple, fractions, Square Root, and simple equations of one unknown quantity, with easy problems which lead to them.

† The same as for the previous year, and cube root, simultaneous equations of the first degree of two unknown quantities, and quadratic equations involving one unknown quantity, with easy problems leading to them.

Geography.

(In Welsh districts in the first year special questions will be set on the physical geography of Wales, and in the second year on the industries of Wales, and maps will be required to illustrate the answers given.)

First Year.—The British Islands, Australia and British North America. Physical Geography of mountains and rivers. Maps of the British Isles.

Second Year.—Europe and British India. Latitude and Longitude. Climate and productions of the British possessions. Maps of France, Italy, and the Spanish Peninsula.

Third Year.—Asia and Africa. Winds and ocean currents. Maps of India, South Africa and the Mediterranean Sea.

Fourth Year.—America and Polynesia. The seasons, the sun, moon, planetary system. The tides. Maps of the United States and Australia.

History.

First Year.—Outlines of British History to the Norman Conquest.

Second Year.—From the Conquest to the accession of the Tudors.

In Welsh districts, Welsh History to the death of Owen Glyndwr.

Third Year.—From the accession of the Tudors to 1688.

In Welsh districts, outlines of English History from the Noman Conquest to the Tudor accession.

Fourth Year.—From 1688 to the present time.

In Welsh districts, general outlines of English History from the Tudor accession to the present time, with special knowledge of the history of Wales during that period.

MUSIC.

Graded tests in tune, time and ear training, based upon the requirements for the various school divisions.

The highest marks will be given to candidates able to sing at sight passages combining the time and tune required above, and to tell ear exercises freely.

1. The test can be sung from the staff notation or from the tonic sol-fa notation, at the option of the candidate.

2. As the application of every test (song, note, time and ear) to first, second and third year pupil teachers may occupy more time than can be given, it will suffice if each candidate is examined in time (the third year in combined time and tune) and one other point.

NOTE.—In all the subjects questions may be given on the work of the previous years, and on the mode of teaching them.

APPENDIX C.

COURSE OF STUDY FOR MALE TEACHERS IN TRAINING COLLEGES IN NORMAL SCHOOLS, ENGLAND.

First Year.

Reading and Repetition from Memory.—To read with a distinct utterance, due attention to the punctuation, and just expression.

The students of the first year and acting teachers taking first year papers will read passages from Scott's "Old Mortality" and Shakespeare's "As You Like It." The Inspector will hear each student and acting teacher read from either of the books prescribed for his year, and also from another book which he may bring or choose.

Each student and acting teacher must have learned, at least, three hundred lines from the works of Milton, Byron, Wordsworth or Tennyson.

Each student will be called upon to repeat some part at the annual inspection of the training college; each acting teacher must do the same at the annual inspection of his school.

Penmanship.—1. To write a specimen of the penmanship used in setting copies of text hand and small hand.

2. To write a passage from dictation.

3. The general character of the writing in the examination papers will be considered in deciding upon the proficiency of candidates in this subject.

School Management.—1. The general principles of teaching.

2. The methods of teaching the elementary and class subjects and drawing. The methods and principles of infant teaching and discipline, and cultivating the intelligence of children.

3. The training of the senses and the memory, and the order in which the faculties of children are developed.

4. Notes of lessons.

Passages taken from Reading Lesson Books commonly used in schools may be given in the papers on all subjects which admit of it, and candidates will be expected to show how they would explain such passages to children. Each paper may also contain questions on the method of teaching the elementary parts of the subject to which it relates

English.—1. Parsing, analysis, and the principles of grammar.

2. An intelligent acquaintance with the language, style, and subject matter of Tennyson's "Gareth and Lynette," and "Geraint and Enid," and Trench's "Study of Words," Lectures IV., V., VI. (thirteenth or any subsequent edition.)

Geography and History.—A candidate who has, at the Queen's Scholarship Examination in one of the two preceding years, passed with exceptional credit in Geography or History, is released from the obligation to take up the subject again at the first year's examination, and may substitute for each subject in which he has so passed a language or a science.

Geography.—1. Elementary knowledge of physical geography, with special reference to:

(*a*) Shape, size, and motions of the earth.
(*b*) The atmosphere, rain, clouds, and vapour.
(*c*) Winds, currents, and tides.
(*d*) Causes which affect climate.
(*e*) Effect of climate on industry, productions, and national character.
(*f*) Distribution of plants and animals.

2. General geography of the Continent of Asia.

Sketch maps, such as should be drawn by a teacher in the illustration lessons, may be required of Hindostan Palestine, and China.

English History.—1. General knowledge of the most memorable events of English History, from 1066 to 1815, and of their immediate causes and effects.

2. The History of England during the eighteenth century with special reference to:

(*a*) Constitutional changes and most important laws.
(*b*) Military and naval operations abroad and at home.
(*c*) The industrial condition of the people.
(*d*) The literature of the period.

Arithmetic, Algebra, and Mensuration.—1. To work arithmetical sums, both mentally and on paper. In arithmetic the use of algebraical symbols in the solution of questions is permitted.

2. To prove and explain the rules.

3. To answer simple questions, both theoretical and practical, in Algebra, and the mensuration of plane surfaces.

Algebra: The four simple rules, involution, evolution, common measures, common multiples, fractions, surds, ratio, proportion, variations, progressions, simple equations, and easy quadratic equations of one or two unknown quantities, and problems leading to such equations.

Mensuration: Plane rectilineal figures, and the circle.

Geometry.—The first three books of Euclid, with simple deductions from the propositions and easy geometrical problems.

Euclid's definitions will be required and no axioms or postulates except Euclid's may be assumed. The actual proofs of propositions as given in Euclid will not be required, but no proof of any proposition occurring in Euclid will be admitted, in which use is made of any proposition which in Euclid's order occurs subsequently.

Languages (Optional):
    1. Latin.   3. French.
    2. Greek.   4. German.

A candidate not exempt from the examination in geography or history may not, in his first year, take up more than two languages or two subjects of science, or one language and one subject of science.

Second Year.

Reading and Repetition from Memory.—To show improvement in the higher qualities of reading, such as expression, modulation of voice, and the correct delivery of long or involved sentences.

The students of the Second Year and Acting Teachers taking second year papers, will read passages from "Wordsworth" (in the "Golden Treasury Series") and "Essays written in the intervals of business," by Sir Arthur Helps. The Inspector will hear each candidate read from either of these books, and also from another book which he may bring or choose.

Each student and Acting teacher must have learned, at least, three hundred lines from a play of Shakespeare. Each student will be called upon to repeat some part at the annual inspection of the training College; and each acting teacher must do the same at the annual inspection of his school.

Penmanship.—As in first year, but defects will be more severely visited with loss of marks.

School Management.—No student will be examined unless the Principal certifies that he has spent, at least one hundred and fifty hours in the Practising Schools under proper superintendence, during the period of training, and at least half of that time during his second year

1. To teach a class in the presence of Her Majesty's Inspector.

2. The different methods of organizing and managing an elementary school.

3. The form of school registers, the mode of keeping them, and of making returns from them.

4. The processes of reasoning; the formation of habits and character; considered in their application to the methods of teaching and of moral discipline.

5. The laws of health as applied to school premises, scholars, and teachers.

6. Notes of lessons.

7. Herbert Spencer on Education, Chapters I. and II., or Quick's "Educational Reformers," Chapters 13, 16, 17, 18.

English.—1. Grammar, analysis, and paraphrase.

2. An intelligent acquaintance with the language, style and subject matter of Shakspeare's "Macbeth," Tennyson's "Gareth and Lynette," and "Geraint and Enid;" and Trench's "Study of Words," Lectures IV., V. and VI. (thirteenth or any subsequent edition.)

Geography (Optional.)—1. Elementary knowledge of physical geography, with special reference to:

(*a*) Shape, size, and motions of the earth.

(*b*) The atmosphere, rain, clouds and vapour.

(*c*) Winds, currents, and tides.

(*d*) Causes which affect climate.

(*e*) Effect of climate on industry, production and national character.

(*f*) Distribution of plants and animals.

2. General geography of the Continent of Asia. Sketch maps, such as should be drawn by a teacher in the illustration of lessons, may be required of Hindostan, Palestine, and China.

English History (Optional.)—1. General knowledge of the most memorable events of English History, from 1066 to 1815, and of their immediate causes and effects.

2. The History of England during the eighteenth century, with special reference to:

(*a*) Constitutional changes and most important laws.

(*b*) Military and naval operations abroad and at home.
(*c*) The industrial condition of the people.
(*d*) The literature of the period.

Languages :

    1. Latin.   3. French.
    2. Greek.   4. German.

Economy (Optional.)—Elementary questions in political economy.

Drawing and Sciences (Optional.)—If a student takes up a science subject in his first year, and fails to pass in it, he must, should he present himself in science at all at the end of his second year, take up the subject in which he failed; but he may drop science altogether in favor of another optional subject.

Third Year.

Teaching a class in the presence of H. M. Inspector.

The art, theory, and history of teaching. (Special subjects to be named from time to time.)

In 1893 and 1894 the special subjects are any two of the following :—" The Life and Work of Dr. Arnold," Quick's " Educational Reformers," Bain's " Education as a Science," "The Teacher's Handbook of Psychology," by Sully.

The candidate will be examined in two of the following four groups :

Group I.—English.— History, literature, and biography (special subjects to be named from time to time.) The special subjects for 1893 and 1894 are :—Hallam's

"Constitutional History," Chapters XIII. to XVIII., inclusive. Southey's " Life of Nelson," Milton's 'Samson Agonistes."

Group II.—Mathematics.—Algebra, Euclid I-IV. and VI., Mensuration, Plane Trigonometry to the end of the solution of triangles, elementary Statics and Elementary Dynamics.

Group III.—Languages.—Two of the four langaages. Latin, Greek, French, German. Easy passages will be given for translation from and into English, with questions on grammar, and on the construction of sentences.

Group IV.—Science.—Two of the sciences included in the syllabus of the Science and Art Department, the student taking the paper in honors. No subject is to be taken up in the third year by a student who has previously obtained honors in that subject.

APPENDIX D.

SYLLABUS OF COURSE IN CIVICS FOR NIGHT SCHOOLS

1. *Life and Duties of the Citizen.*—"It is our business carefully to cultivate in our minds, to rear to the most perfect vigour and maturity, every sort of generous and honest feeling that belongs to our nature. To bring the dispositions that are lovely in private life into the service and conduct of the commonwealth ; so to be patriots as not to forget we are gentlemen. . . Public life is a situation of power and energy ; he trespasses against his duty who sleeps upon his watch, as well as he that goes over to the enemy."—Burke's Thoughts on the Cause of the Present Discontents.

Explanatory Note.

[This syllabus touches only on certain limited aspects of the public life of the citizen. Various important considerations are therefore omitted, which teachers will no doubt discuss in dealing with the subject.

The subject as here set out will be found difficult to teach, except to those older scholars who are in the habit of reading and thinking intelligently about public affairs. For the instruction of such students the general outline here given, may be of service to teachers, though it covers more ground than can be dealt with even in two or three courses. The teacher will select that part which is more appropriate to the circumstances and needs of the school and the locality. For younger scholars a much simpler form of syllabus should be prepared from which the more technical treatment of the machinery of Local and Central Government should be omitted.

The object of the teacher should be to proceed from the known and familiar, such as the policeman, the rate collector, the board of guardians, and the town council, to the history of, and reasons for our local and national institutions and our responsibilities in connexion with them.

Good illustrations and diagrams and pictures will be of great service in teaching this subject.]

INTRODUCTORY.

What the citizen should aim at in the interest of his country.

Public duties accompany all forms of work in life, whatever the occupation or profession. Serving personal interest alone is not enough.

The individual benefits from a well-ordered community. The community ought to benefit in its turn from the efforts of the individual. "All for each" should be requited by "each for all."

The reasons for attachment to our country and for a sense of duty towards our fellow citizens are similar to those for love of home and family. Loyalty to one's own village or town should lead to a larger patriotism. Those who are growing up into citizenship should realize their debt to the men and women who have served the nation generously and wisely in the past, and their own duty to their country in the present. Self interest and class interest should be subordinate to general and national interests

---

The Nation and the State.—What they mean.—Difference between Representative Government and Despotic Government.—Responsibilities involved in Representative Government.

1.—REPRESENTATIVE GOVERNMENT.

What representative institutions mean. The co-operation of the people in the work of the Government. The power of the majority; its limits. The force of public opinion. Need of public spirit and of intelligence for good government.

The machinery of government is partly local, partly central.

A.—*Local Government.*

Local Government Districts, Small and Large. Institutions of Local Self Government.

1. The Village and the Parish.—The Vestry. The choosing of overseers, Guardians, etc.

2. School Districts.—School Boards, School Managers and School Attendance Committees.

3. The Poor Law Union.—Boards of Guardians.

4. Local Board Districts.—Boroughs and Counties, Local Boards, Town Councils and County Councils. The choosing of Mayors, Aldermen and Councillors.

Composition and methods of election of bodies above mentioned.

Work and Powers of these Bodies as regards :

1. Rating and Expenditure.—The Rate Collector. Purposes for which money is spent. Difference between rating and taxation.

2. Health.—Sanitary condition of houses; drainage, baths and wash-houses; gas; water; purification of rivers. Hospitals; sick nursing. Sanitary and medical officers.

3. Education.—Day and Evening Continuation Schools. Provision of schools and attendance at school. School attendance officers. Free libraries. Picture galleries and museums. Technical education.

4. The Destitute Poor.—The relieving officer. Outdoor and indoor relief. The workhouse.

5. Roads, Streets, Buildings and Land.—Paving and lighting of streets. Public parks and recreation grounds. Town halls and municipal buildings. What goes on inside them. Purchase of land for improvements and public purposes. Allotments and small holdings.

6. Police and Justice.—The policeman, his powers and duties. The magistrate, how appointed; his powers and duties. Petty sessions and quarter sessions. Public houses and licensing.

The local representative bodies have in most cases certain responsibilities to or dealings with the Central Government (see B iii Executive Government).

B.—Central Government.

i. The Crown and the two Houses of Parliament.

(1) The Crown.—Its constitutional position and powers.

(2) House of Lords.
    (*a*) Composition.
    (*b*) Powers.
(3) House of Commons.
    (*a*) Composition. How members of Parliament are elected. The franchise and the ballot.
    (*b*) Powers.
(4) Working of the Parliamentary System.—Taxation, legislation, administration. Party Government. Ministry and Cabinet—their joint responsibility. Ministry and Opposition. Majorities and Minorities. Their powers. How a Bill becomes an Act of Parliament.

ii. The Judicial System.—Justice.—The Lord Chancellor. Judges. Magistrates. Coroners. How appointed. Courts of Law. Civil and criminal. Petty Sessions, Quarter Sessions, County Courts, Assizes, High Court, Court of Appeal, House of Lords. Privy Council. Juries and their relation to Courts of Law.

iii. Executive Government.—The duty of carrying into effect many of the laws, and the decisions of Parliament from time to time, is entrusted to various public departments, the most important of which are presided over by responsible Ministers of the Crown.

The Work and Powers of the Executive Government:

(1) In connection with the work of representative Local Bodies in matters of Education, Health and the destitute Poor. (Education Department and Local Government Board.)

(2) In matters of Trade, Commerce, Agriculture, Post Office, Telegraphs and Savings' Banks. (Board of Trade, Board of Agriculture, Post Office.)

(3) In matters of Labour (see under III.) (Home Office, Board of Trade.)

(4) In matters of Justice. Prisons and Police. (Home Office.)

(5) In connection with Scotland and Ireland. (Scotch Office and Irish Office.)

(6) In connection with the Colonies, India and Foreign Countries (see II. the Empire). (Colonial Office, India Office, Foreign Office.)

(7) In connection with the Army and Navy. (War Office, Admiralty.) The army; the army reserve, militia, yeomanry and volunteers. The navy; naval reserve; coast guards. Duties and responsibilities of the soldiers and sailors of the country by land and sea. The evils of war. Efforts that have been made to avert it by arbitration.

(8) In matters of Taxation and Finance. (The Treasury.) The country's yearly Bill. What we pay for. How the money is got. Direct and indirect taxation.

C.—Duties of Citizens in relation to Local and Central Government.

1. Right and duty of voting.—Different kinds of votes. Need of honesty in given a vote. The vote a "trust" as well as a "right." Each vote has a special end and aim, which ought to be considered. The gain and loss of party spirit.

2. Rates and Taxes, and what we get in return for them. Reasons for willingness to contribute to common purposes in well administered countries. Illustrations of gain to the community from improved conditions of life and health as a result of rates and taxes well spent.

3. Public Health.—Attention to sanitary matters at home, cleanliness and ventilation. Isolation and disinfection in illness ; temperance and temperate habits ; duty to neighbors as well as home and family. Healthiness of a district; its value to the community. Public parks, gardens and open spaces. Duty of making them beautiful and taking good care of them.

4. Education.—Duty of parents. To enforce regularity of attendance, to co-operate with the teacher in regard to conduct of scholars, to home lessons, and the care and use of books.

Duty of scholars. To make full use of the advantages of the school, and thus fit themselves to become capable and useful citizens.

Influence of school on character as well as on intelligence. Waste of force and money through leaving school too early. Techinical education, its value for the worker. Higher education and the Universities. School and College only the beginning of the citizen's education.

5. Provision for the Poor.—Care of poor children and the sick and aged poor. Consideration of the causes of pauperism, and how to diminish it. Importance of self-dependence and habits of providence.

6. Need of Order and Respect for Law.—The citizen's home and protection. Respect for the persons, opinions, property and reputation of others. Discouragement of fraud in all relations of life and business. Support of the law and encouragement by example of peaceable behaviour by all citizens. Examples of what the law

demands, (*a*) Registration of births, deaths and marriages. (*b*) Notification of infectious diseases. (*c*) Prevention of cruelty to children and to animals.

7. Public Spirit and Public Opinion.—Force of public opinion; need of honesty and intelligence. Freedom of speech and writing. Uses of public meetings; how they should be conducted. Watchfulness over public bodies. Services of the public press in these matters. Active co-operation of the whole body of the people essential to good government and freedom. Willingness of capable persons to serve in a representative capacity on public bodies of great importance.

II.—The Empire.

Great Britain and Ireland. "Greater Britain."—The Colonies. Variety of Races in Colonies and dependencies. Self-governing Colonies. Crown Colonies. Protectorates. India and its government.

Imperial coinage and Imperial postage.

Appointment of Governors General and Governors.

Obligation to cultivate knowledge about our brethren "across the sea." Native races within the Empire, and our duties to them.

Extension of friendly feeling, and of courtesy and fair dealing towards foreign nations. Appointment of Ambassadors, Envoys, and Consuls.

III.—Industrial and Social Life and Duties.

Selection for boys or girls of work in life. Loss to the nation when they are set to uncongenial labour. Corresponding gain of "tools to the men who can use them."

What constitutes national wealth. Every capable and industrious and self-respecting citizen should add to the wealth of the community. Relation of skill and knowledge: (*a*) to personal well-being and happiness; (*b*) to industrial success; (*c*) to power of public usefulness.

The great industries of the country, their growth and development.

Changes caused by the use of machinery.

Associations of Workers:

1. Trade unions, their history and work. Labour disputes and strikes. Arbitration and conciliation.

2. Co-operative societies; their work in distribution and production.

3. Friendly societies. Training in habits of industry; thrift and self help.

Value of the work of voluntary associations in the education of the adult citizen.

The State and Labour.—Factory Acts; Mines Acts; Women's and Children's labour; Dangerous employments; Health and safety of the worker.

Information as to condition of workers. Labour Department of Board of Trade.

The Government and Municipalities as employers of labour. Dockyards, Arsenals, and public works.

The importance to the nation of effective, honest, and intelligent management of all forms of business and industry. The disasters which result from mismanagement or fraud.

The duty of the community to sympathize with every reasonable effort of the workers to improve their condition, and develop their intelligence. That which injures their efficiency or lessons their hopefulness leads to national loss, and to the maintenance or increase of poverty and ignorance. A healthy and skilful body of workers, upright in character and self-reliant, is a source of strength to the country.

Faithful discharge of homelier duties of life is the best preparation for their discharge in city and nation. Civic duty begins in the life of the family; expands with occupation in trade, business, and profession.

In earning their livelihood men and women also serve their fellow citizens, and their country. Membership of self-governing societies is among the best means of civic education.

As intelligence, honour, and virtue are essential to the welfare of the family, so is patriotism necessary to national and social life. We have to recognize that our public responsibilities are duties as much as personal and family obligations. We have no right to expect just legislation or impartial administration unless we perform with intelligence those public duties which devolve upon all. If we suffer injustice in connection with public affairs, we have little right to complain unless we have done our own duty.

APPENDIX E.

RULES TO BE OBSERVED IN PLANNING AND FITTING UP PUBLIC ELEMENTARY SCHOOLS.

Requirements.

School Boards and School Promoters are requested to note that the Education Department require the following Plans, and that inattention to such requirement entails delay:—

I.—A Block Plan of the Site, drawn to a scale of 20 feet to an inch.

This plan must indicate:—

(*a*) The position of the school buildings.

(*b*) Out-buildings.

(*c*) Play-ground.

(*d*) Drains (collateral and main), with their fall and depth below ground.

(*e*) Entrances.

(*f*) Boundary walls, or fences, and their nature.

(*g*) Roads.

(*h*) The points of the compass.

(*i*) The levels of the ground at the principal points.

II.—A Plan of each Floor of the Schoolrooms (and Teacher's or Caretaker's Residence, if any) drawn to a scale of 8 feet to an inch. The internal fittings of the rooms (fire-places, groups of desks, benches, &c.) must be accurately shown. The plan should also state whether the rooms are intended for boys, girls or infants. In cases of enlargement, a plan showing the buildings as they exist is needed.

III.—Sections and at least four Elevations, also shown to a scale of 8 feet to an inch. The ceiling, the positions of window-heads in relation thereto, and the mode of ventilation must be shown.

N. B.—(*a*) Pencil drawings cannot be received, but coloured tracings in ink may be submitted while plans are in the preliminary stage of pencil, so that suggested alterations can be adopted without difficulty or expense.
(*b*) Tracings should be on cloth.
(*c*) In the case of enlargements, the whole site and existing building should be accurately shown.
(*d*) All plans should be dated, the scales drawn on, and dimensions figured.

IV.—A detailed Specification separated under the several branches of the Building Trade.

Building Rules.

1.—PLANNING AND ACCOMMODATION.

1. In planning a school, the first thing is to seat the children in the best manner for being taught. The accommodation of each room depends not merely on its area, but also on its shape (especially in relation to the

kind of desk proposed), the position of the doors and fireplaces, and its proper lighting. The second point is to group the rooms together in a compact and convenient manner.

2. AND 3.—SCHOOLROOMS.

2. Every school must have a schoolroom as hereunder or a central hall as under Rule 8. The proper width for a schoolroom is 18 to 20 feet for long desks, or 22 feet for dual desks. If the width does not exceed 20 feet, groups of long desks, three or four in number, according to the width, must be used; if the width is 22 feet, dual desks, five rows deep, must be used. (For class-rooms, see Rule 7.)

(*a*) Accommodation in schoolrooms for elder children is calculated by the number of children seated at desks and benches, subject to a minimum of 10 square feet per child being provided. For the mode of calculating accommodation in classrooms, see Rule 7, in infant schools see Rule 16.

(*b*) Double bank schools (now almost obsolete) require rooms 32 feet wide, walls left clear for three rows of desks, and ample lighting from windows on both sides extending to ceiling.

(*c*) Wasted space cannot be considered.

3. The doors and fireplaces in school-rooms must be so placed as to allow of the whole of one side of the schoolroom being left free for the groups of benches and desks.

(*a*) No school-room lighted from one side only can be approved. The gable ends should be fully utilized for light. (See also Rules 9 and 9 (*b*).)

14

4.—Walls, Floors, and Roofs.

4. The walls of every school-room and class-room, if cciled at the level of the wall-plate, must be at least 12 feet high from the level of the floor to the ceilling; and, if the area contain more than 360 superficial square feet, 13 feet, and, if more than 600, then 14 feet.

(*a*) The walls of every school-room and class-room, if ceiled to the rafters and collar beam, must be at least 11 feet high from the floor to the wall-plate, and at least 14 feet to the ceiling across the collar beam.

(*b*) Great care should be taken to render the roofs impervious to cold and heat.

(*c*) Roofs open to the apex are not approved. They can only be permitted where the roofs are specially impervious to heat and cold, and where apex-ventilation is provided. Iron tie-rods are least unsightly when placed horizontally.

(*d*) The whole of the external walls of the school and residence must be solid. If of brick, the thickness must be at least one brick and a half; and if of stone, at least 20 inches.

(*e*) All walls, not excepting fence walls, must have a damp-proof course just above the ground line.

(*f*) The whole area of the building should have concrete 6 inches thick under the ground floor, and air bricks for ventilation to joists.

(*g*) Timber should be protected from mortar and cement by asphalt or tar.

5.—Entrances.

5. Entrances should be separate for each department. In large schools more than one entrance is desirable.

The principal entrances should never be through the cloak-room. Entrance doors should open outwards. A porch should be external to the school-room.

6.—Cloak-Rooms.

6. Cloak-rooms must be external to school-rooms and class-rooms with gangways at least 4 feet wide, amply lighted from the end. Hat-pegs should be 12 inches apart, numbered, and of two tiers. The hanging-space should be 6 inches lineal per child so as to provide a separate peg for each.

7.—Class-Rooms.

7. Class-rooms are calculated at 10 square feet if not providing accommodation for more than 60 children.

Six rows of dual desks or four rows of long-length desks are permissible in such class-rooms. Rule 2 applies to all rooms providing accommodation for more than 60, or being more than 24 feet 8 inches deep from the window wall.

(*a*) The minimum size of class-room is 18 feet x 15 feet. If desks are placed longitudinally the width should not be less than 16 feet. This latter width is also allowed in school-rooms of very small size.

(*b*) The class-rooms should never be passage-rooms from one part of the building to another, nor from the school-rooms to the play-ground or yard, and should be on the same level as the school-room. Each should be easily cleared without disturbance to any other room.

(*c*) The number of class-rooms should, where practicable, equal the number of classes in the school-room.

(*d*) The excessive use of movable partitions should be avoided.

8.—HALLS.

8. Large schools are sometimes planned with a central hall, which is not calculated in the accommodation.

In the case of mixed schools an exception is made, one class being necessary in the hall in order to secure a teacher's supervision of the separate exits to the latrines (see Rule 13, (*a*) the hall must, therefore, be suitable for teaching such class, it must be fully lighted, warmed, and ventilated, and must contain a floor space of not less than 1,200 square feet, and the fittings must be marked on the plan.

9.—WINDOWS.

9. The light should, as far as possible, and especially in class-rooms, be admitted from the left side of the scholars. (This rule will be found greatly to influence the planning.) All other windows in class-rooms should be regarded as supplementary, or for summer ventilation. In cases where left light is impossible, right light is next best. Windows full in the eyes of teachers or scholars are not approved. In rooms fourteen feet high any space beyond twenty-four feet from the window wall is insufficiently lighted.

(*a*) Windows should never be provided for the sake merely of external effect. All kinds of glazing which diminish the light and are troublesome to keep clean and in repair, should be avoided. A large portion of each window should be made to open for ventilation and for cleaning.

(*b*) The sills of the main lighting windows should be placed about four feet above the floor. And the tops of some should always reach nearly to the ceiling. The ordinary rules respecting hospitals should here be remembered.

(c) Skylights are objectionable and should never be resorted to where windows are possible. Plans necessarily involving their use cannot be approved, except in the case on central halls having ridge, or apex, ventilation.

10.—STAIRCASES.

10. A staircase like a porch must be external to the school room. No triangular steps or "winders" should be used. Each step should be about thirteen inches broad and not more than six inches high. The flights should be short and the landing unbroken by steps. The number of staircases should be sufficient, not only for daily use, but for rapid exit in case of fire or panic.

11.—VENTILATION.

11. Apart from open windows and doors, there should be provision for copious inlet of fresh air; also for outlet of foul air at the highest point of the room; the best way for providing the latter is to build to each room a separate air chimney carried up in the same stack with smoke flues. An outlet should be warmed in some manner or it will frequently act as a cold inlet. The principal point in all ventilation is to prevent stagnant air. Particular expedients are only subsidiary to this main direction.

(a) Although lighting from the left hand is considered so importaant, ventilation in summer demands also the provision of a small swing window as far from the lighting as possible and near the ceiling.

12.—Warming.

12. The warming should be moderate and evenly distributed so as to maintain a temperature of from 56° to 60°. When a corridor or lobby is warmed the rooms are more easily dealt with, and are less liable to cold draughts. Where schools are wholly warmed by hot water, the principle of direct radiation is recommended. In such cases open grates in addition are useful for extra warming occasionally, and their flues for ventilation always.

(a) A common stove, with a pipe through the wall or roof, can under no circumstances be allowed. Stoves are only approved when

>   (I.) Provided with proper chimneys (as in the case of open fires);
>
>   (II.) Of such a pattern that they cannot become red-hot or otherwise contaminate the air;
>
>   (III.) Supplied with fresh air, direct from the outside, by a flue of not less than 72 inches superficial, and
>
>   (IV.) Not of such size or shape as to interfere with the floor space necessary for teaching purposes.

(b) A thermometer should always be kept hung up in a school.

13.—Sanitary Arrangements.

13. Water-closets within the main school building are not desirable, and are only sanctioned for female teachers. All others should be a short distance and completely disconnected from the school.

(*a*) The doors, staircases, and passages leading from the school room to the latrines (whether in mixed or in other schools), and the latrines themselves, must be separate for the two sexes and constructed entirely apart from each other. In the case of a mixed school the rule especially affects the planning.

(*b*) Each closet must be separate, having a door and ventilation to each. More than one set is not allowed in any closet. A good light should be provided.

(*c*) The children must not be allowed to pass in front of the teacher's residence in order to reach their latrines.

(*d*) The following table shows approximately the number of closets needed:

	For Girls.	For Boys.
Under 50 children	3	2
" 70 "	4	2
" 100 "	5	3
" 150 "	6	3
" 200 "	7	4
" 300 "	8	5*

*Urinals in proportion.

(*e*) Cesspools and privies should only be used when unavoidable. Earth or ash closets of an approved type may be employed in rural districts, but drains for the disposal of slop and surface water are still necessary.

(*f*) Soil-drains must always be laid outside the building (on a hard even bottom or concrete) in straight lines with glazed stoneware pipes, carefully jointed in cement and made absolutely water-tight. A diameter of 4 inches is sufficient unless for drains receiving the discharge of more than ten closets. Above this number the diameter should be 6 inches. The fall should never be less than 1 in 30 for 4-inch and 1 in 40 for 6-inch drains. An inspection opening or chamber should be provided at each change of direction so as to facilitate cleaning the drain without opening the ground. Every soil-drain must be disconnected from the main sewer by a properly constructed trap placed on the line of drain between the latrines and the public sewer. This trap must be thoroughly ventilated by at least two untrapped openings; one being the 4-inch soil pipe carried up full size above the roof, and the other an inlet pipe connected with the side of the trap furthest from the public sewer. Automatic flushing tanks are desirable where trough closets are used.

(*g*) Urinals must in all cases have a sufficient supply of water for flushing.

(*h*) Waste pipes from sinks or lavatories should be first trapped inside and then made to discharge direct through the wall over a trapped gulley.

14.—DESKS.

14. Benches and desks, graduated according to the ages of the children, should be provided for all the scholars and placed at right angles to the light. (See also Rules 3 (*a*) and 9.)

An allowance of 18 inches per scholar at each desk and bench will suffice (except in the case of the dual desk), and the length of each group should therefore be some multiple of 18 inches, with gangways of 18 inches between the groups and at the walls. In the case of the dual desk the usual length is 3' 4", and the gangways 1' 4"

(*a*) The desk should be very slightly inclined. An angle of 15° is sufficient. The objections to the inclined desk are, that pencils, pens, etc., are constantly slipping from it, and that it cannot be conveniently used as a table. The objection to the flat desk is, that it has a tendency to make the children stoop. A raised ledge in front of a desk interferes with the arm in writing.

(*b*) As a general rule, no benches and desks should be more than 12 feet long. And no group of long desks, in a school room providing for more than 60 children, should contain more than four rows of benches and desks (or three if the width is less than 20 feet) because in proportion as the depth is increased the teacher must raise his voice to a higher pitch; and thus becomes exhausting to himself, while at the same time it adds inconveniently to the general noise.

15.—Sites and Playgrounds.

15. Every school should have an open, airy playground, proportioned to the size and need of the school. The minimum size of site is, in the absence of exceptional circumstances, a quarter of an acre for every 250 children. If the school is of more than one storey this area may be proportionately reduced. The minimum open space is 30 square feet per child.

(*a*) In the case of a mixed school, playgrounds must be separate for the boys and girls.

(*b*) All playgrounds should be properly levelled, drained, inclosed and fitted with some simple appliances A portion should be covered, having one side against a wall. A covered way should never connect the offices with the main building. Buttresses and corners should be avoided.

(*c*) An infant school should have its playground on the same level as the school.

16.—INFANT SCHOOLS.

16. Infants should not, except in very small schools, be taught in the same room with older children, as the noise and the training of the infants disturb and injuriously affect the discipline and instruction of the other children.

(*a*) There must be no opening wider than an ordinary doorway between an infants' and any other school room, because of the sound of the infant teaching.

(*b*) An infant school and playground should always be on the ground floor, and if more than eighty scholars are admitted, should have one gallery and a small group of benches and desks for the occasional use of the elder infants.

(*c*) No infant gallery should hold more than eighty or ninety infants. It should be well lighted from one side. The light for object lessons is as good from the right as from the left.

(*d*) The width of an infant school room should be in proportion to its size, but not more than twenty-four feet.

(*e*) The babies' room should always have an open fire

(*f*) The accommodation of an infant school is calculated at eight square feet for each child, after deducting wasted or useless space, but a larger area should be allowed wherever practicable. Where a Second Standard is taken in an infant school the accommodation for it is calculated at ten square feet per child.

17.—COOKERY CENTRES AND CLASS-ROOMS.

17. A cookery centre should be capable of accommodating at least one class of twenty-four at practice and not more than seventy-two at demonstration at one time. A cookery class-room should contain about four hundred superficial feet, and be approached by a separate entrance in the girls' playground. A small scullery is necessary.

18.—WORKSHOPS AND LAUNDRIES.

18. Workshops and laundries are best entirely apart from the school.

19.—TEACHER'S HOUSE, ETC.

19. The residence for the master or mistress should contain a parlour, a kitchen, a scullery and three bedrooms; and the smallest dimensions which their Lordships can approve are:

For the parlour...12 ft. by 12 ft.	of superficial area.	8 feet	in height to wall plate.
For the kitchen...12 ft. by 10 ft.		8 feet	
For one of the bedrooms ....12 ft. by 10 ft.			
For two other bedrooms .... 9 ft. by 8 ft.		8 feet if ceiled at wall plate, and 9 feet to ceiling.	

(*a*) The residence must be so planned that the staircase is immediately accessible from an entrance-lobby and from the parlour, kitchen and each bedroom, without making a passage of any room.

(*b*) Each bedroom must be on the upper storey, and must have a fireplace.

(*c*) The parlour must not open directly into the kitchen or scullery.

(*d*) There must be no internal communication between the residence and the school.

(*e*) There must be a separate and distinct yard, with offices.

(*f*) A caretaker's house need not be quite so large.

(*g*) All houses should be separate from and not built as part of the schoolhouse.

20 and 21 Loans.

20. No loan of money can be obtained from the Public Works Loan Commissioners unless the whole cost of the school, exclusive of site, legal expenses, extra rooms for instruction authorized by the code, and residences (if any), is kept within the sum of £10 per child accommodated. An allowance will also be made in reference to the cost of a Central Hall not calculated in the accommodation (rule 8). Rooms for extra subjects recognized by the New Code, such as Drawing, Chemistry, etc., will have an allowance varying from 15s. to 20s. per square foot. From £275 to £400 will be allowed for a caretaker's house. From £275 to £500 will be allowed for a cookery centre. Whether the necessary loan be borrowed in the open market or not, extravagant plans cannot be approved.

21. The Department do not entertain applications for loans when the expenditure has been incurred without their previous sanction.

APPENDIX F.

SYLLABUS OF WORK IN GERMAN ELEMENTARY SCHOOLS.

INTRODUCTORY REMARKS.

Teachers should prepare themselves for all lessons, the younger teachers especially with pen in hand. All work of pupils should be most conscientiously controlled.

SYLLABUS OF WORK.

(a) Religious instruction (not given).

LANGUAGE WORK (GERMAN).

The pupils should be taught to speak and write correctly. Special attention should be given to letters and common business forms. A taste for good reading should be cultivated.

(c) *Object Teaching.*—Lowest Division.—Pupils should be led to talk about objects which are brought to their notice. The teacher is to correct, carefully, faulty enunciation and incorrect expression. Instruction in reading and writing should follow the system taught in the Normal School of the district. The alphabet method is absolutely forbidden. After six months' instruction pupils should be able to divide simple statements into words, the words into syllables, and the syllables into their respective sounds. They must be able to make and read each letter according to its sound.

At the close of six months the children are made acquainted with the printed characters and the names of the letters.

When children learn to read, they should be taught to associate words, and then statements, with the object or idea represented, to prevent thoughtless, mechanical reading.

The pieces read should be thoroughly understood by the pupils. The principal thoughts are best brought out by questions on the part of the teacher.

In addition to short proverbs, aphorisms, etc., the pupils should learn by heart some short selections from the primer. They should also have practice in repeating in their own words, what they have read.

The children of this division learn also the Roman printed characters.

In teaching writing, the teacher explains the formation of the letters upon the blackboard.

Before leaving this third and lowest division, the pupils should be able to read with facility, correct enunciation and expression the selections they have had. They should be able to answer questions as to what they have read; reproduce all selections in their own words, and copy correctly from the primer. They should also have had some exercise in writing at Dictation.

Middle Class.—Further practice in reading, with more careful attention to subject-matter and expression.

Writing must now be taken at fixed hours, the pupils using partly pen and ink.

Pupils are now to learn the formation of the plural nouns. Statements are made embracing nouns in the singular and plural numbers. Pupils learn to recognize and employ in statements verbs and adjectives. Next come the declensions of nouns, with the definite and indefinite articles, the comparison of adjectives, tenses and moods of verbs. All this work should be taken up very simply and only through many practical examples. Pupils should be taught to transpose simple sentences, and to recognize the principal parts of simple sentences.

The pupils are now ready for simple work in composition. The teacher chooses a subject, generally connected with school work, writes a short outline upon the blackboard, and the pupils complete the same, first orally and then in writing.

Before promotion to the advanced class, pupils should be able to repeat in their own words, the substance of the selections they have read; to read the same with facility, both in the German and Roman characters, to write correctly a simple exercise at dictation, and to reproduce in writing, in their own words, any simple selection which has been taken up in the class.

Advanced Class.—In reading about thirty selections annually are studied so carefully that the children understand well both form and subject-matter. Pupils should be taught to reproduce selections read in correct and logical order.

A number of poems, particularly Volkslieder, songs of the people, should be learned by heart, and repeated until fixed in memory.

Before leaving the school all pupils should be able to read readily and understandingly even difficult articles which, in subject matter, are not too foreign to their line of vision.

Orthography and punctuation are taught by repeated and constant practice in reading, dictation, and composition. Should special faults often occur, the teacher learns thereby to what he should devote most particularly the attention of the class. It is necessary to drill the pupils repeatedly upon words alike in form and sound, and upon the most common foreign words used in German. This is best done by the composition of sentences, showing at the same time both the meaning and the orthography of the words in question.

Fixed hours are appointed for the perfection of the pupils in German and Latin script. It is advisable to select for this purpose proverbs of the people and ordinary business forms.

Pupils must learn to write neatly, legibly and in good form. Pains must be taken with all written work.

The different forms of sentences are taught, with special regard to punctuation. Pupils are drilled on parts of speech and in the analysis of sentences.

Examples are taken, so far as possible, from selections the pupils have read.

Composition, as in the middle class, is continued by exercises in reproduction. Subjects are chosen connected with the curriculum.

The pupils are often asked to write, at the close of lesson, what has been learned in Geography, Natural History, History of the Fatherland, etc.

Written solutions of problems in Arithmetic are often required. Letters must be prepared ready to post. Repeated drill upon ordinary business forms, receipts, notes, etc., is ordered.

Before graduation pupils have considerable practice in original composition.

ARITHMETIC.

The pupils should acquire a thorough knowledge of practical business Arithmetic. They must be trained to give reasons for steps in the solution of problems. Mechanical work must be avoided. Pupils should be most carefully drilled in the system in coinage, weights and measures of the mother country. Problems should be practical. The teacher should avoid long rows of figures beyond the comprehension of the pupils, and take up only that which will be of use to them in trade or in everyday life.

In introducing a new process, in all classes mental should precede written work.

Lowest Class.—The figures from one to ten ; use of objects, marks, points, crosses, etc. ; the numerical frame ; the four fundamental processes, from one to ten ; gradually extended to 100 ; a great variety of simple problems, embracing the numbers from one to 100.

Middle Class.—The figures up to 1,000. The four processes are exercised by problems in mental arithmetic up to 1,000, especially, however, up to 200 ; the pupils learn system of coinage, weights and measures. Practice in written work beyond the number of 1,000.

Advanced Class.—Common and decimal fractions. In common fractions, children should be drilled particularly in those which come up in everyday life (one-half to one-twelfth). Special care should be taken in teaching the reduction of common to decimal fractions, and this method of solution of problems involving unusual common fractions is recommended. Computations of time, ratio and proportion, percentage, interest, profit and loss, discount, partnership, alligation, area of surfaces and contents of solids.

GEOMETRY.

Advanced Class.—This instruction should be connected with drawing on the one hand and arithmetic on the other. By the former, pupils learn to represent correctly, lines, surfaces and solids; by the latter, they understand how to compute the length of lines, the area of surfaces, and the contents of solids.

This instruction should be practical, tending to meet the needs of tradesmen and farmers. It should be given in a simple manner.

The course includes lines, angles, triangles, quadrilaterals, polygons, circles and the regular solid bodies.

DRAWING.

Training of the eye and of the hand is the object of the course in drawing. A taste for symmetry, regularity and beauty of form should be developed. Instruction should be practical, the aim being to afford assistance to those especially who will learn a trade.

Middle Class.—Drawing begins in the middle class, and consists entirely of mechanical work, with the slate, rule and pencil, in copying lines and figures placed upon the blackboard by the teacher.

Advanced Class.—This work is continued with paper and pencil. The pupils now begin free-hand drawing. The school-room, school-house, play-ground, the home, maps of the city or village and district furnish the material for mechanical and free-hand drawing. Pupils who have a special talent for drawing should be allowed to push their work further than the rest of the class.

Industrial drawing and space teaching demands special attention.

The realien include Geography, History and Natural History.

Geography.

The children should be made acquainted with the home, the Fatherland, the German Empire and the principal countries of the earth. They learn the position of the Continents and the principal heavenly bodies. Instruction in Geography is principaly synthetic. It must be studied through representations of the teacher upon the blackboard, through maps, charts, and globes.

Middle Class.—Instruction begins in this class with a description of the school-house, the home and the district. Next comes the Government District, and then the Province. The pupils learn also the boundaries of the Fatherland, the Provinces, with principal cities, the chief rivers and mountains.

Advanced Class.—Review of what has been learned in the middle class. Special attention is now paid to Prussia, the Great Empire and Austria. Other European countries are next studied. Pupils learn name, position, boundaries, the most important rivers, mountains and cities.

The geographical position, boundaries, chief cities, mountains and rivers of other important countries of the world are taken up, more especially those countries which, through their history, culture or commerce, occupy prominent positions.

In Mathematical Geography, the following instruction is recommended.

1. Touching the horizon.
2. Touching representations of the earth, and the significance of the most important lines and points.
3. Touching the form and shape of the earth.
4. Touching the motions of the earth.
5. Touching the seasons and zones.
6. Touching the fixed stars.
7. Touching the sun and moon.
8. Touching the calendar.

History—This instruction includes the history of Prussia and the German Empire. The aim of this instruction is to develop patriotism and loyalty towards the royal family. Instruction in History is given by the teacher in the form of talks. History and Geography should go hand in hand.

Middle Class.—The children learn the names of the Emperor and Empress, the Crown-Prince, and the most important men of the day. The teacher relates anecdotes of these men, and remarkable periods of their lives.

The pupils are next made acquainted with the chief events in the reigns of Frederick, William IV., and Frederick William III. The great men of these reigns are held up to the pupils with their peculiar traits.

Advanced Class.—Instruction is given in the early history of Germany and Brandenburg. Here, only the most remarkable events are touched upon. From the time of the Thirty Years' War, however, instruction is systematic and connected.

In addition to the above, some of the most important inventions and discoveries both in ancient and modern times are taken up.

Natural History.—The aim of this instruction is to acquaint the children with those phenomena in nature which are daily before their eyes. It is one of the most important duties of the teacher to awaken an interest in nature, to train the powers of observation, that the pupils see how much cause for reflection is given by her products and the workings of her forces.

This instruction in natural history should follow the object method. Practical experiments, when possible, are to be most highly commended.

The Middle and Advanced Classes receive together two hours a week of instruction in Natural History.

Middle Class.—In Summer the children learn some of the important plants of the garden, the fields, and the woods. In teaching, the teacher should have before him the plant itself, or a good representation of the same.

In the Winter, the children study some of the Mammalia and Birds, usually the domestic animals.

A few minerals of the district are taken up.

Advanced Class—*Physiology and Hygiene.*—The structure of the human body and the fundamental laws of health. Knowledge of plants, animals and minerals is extended.

In the vegetable kingdom, the most important are fruit-trees, grains and the ordinary vegetables used for food. Useful trees, shrubs, herbs, and poisonous plants are studied. Growth and conditions of growth of plants require attention, as do also the cultivation and fertilization of the field.

Foreign and domestic products, such as cotton, tea, coffee and sugar should be studied.

The proper division of the vegetable kingdom for the Elementary Schools is into (1) trees, (2) shrubs, (3) herbs, (4) grasses, (5) mushrooms, (6) mosses.

The animals studied by the children are brought under the following classification—(1) mammalia, (2) aves, (3) amphibia, (4) fishes, (5) insects, (6) worms, (7) mollusks, (8) infusoria. Foreign words are seldom used in classification.

The animals worthy of special consideration are those useful or dangerous to man; those which by size, construction or peculiarities awaken a high degree of interest. Examples—the butterfly, bee, ant, tape-worm, trichina.

Middle Class.—In nature, the pupils take up the most important peculiarities of air, heat, water, vapor, fog, clouds, dew, frost, rain, snow, hail, ice and storms.

The practical application of natural forces is considered, as in the gun, pumps, etc.

Advanced Class.—In this division are studied the barometer, fountains and water-conduit; the ear, echo, musical instruments; the thermometer, steam engine, manufacture of gas; the effects of light and shade ; colors, the mirror, the burning-glass, eye-glass, the eye and sight. the rainbow; the pully, the lever, the scales, gravitation.

Electricity and Magnetism are taught in connection with the most common applications of these forces. Pupils are given a general idea of the electric telegraph. All this work is to be treated by the object method in a simple manner.

Music.

Vocal Music is an important factor in education. It enobles character by cultivating a taste for that which is beautiful. The pupil takes with him into life a number of songs, which will not only be a source of pleasure to him through life, but will also tend to lesson the influence of corrupt popular songs upon the general public. With this end in view, the greatest care should be taken in the selection of the songs to be learned in school. The preference should be given to those songs which awaken a love of the Fatherland.

Lowest Class.—Exercises to train the voice and ear. The children learn to sing after the teacher, distinct tones in the middle register to the different vowels. The pentachord, both rising and falling, is practiced to various texts. The text of songs is read aloud by the teacher and explained. The pupils then learn the same by heart. A few simple songs should be well studied in this division.

Middle and Advanced Classes.—Continuation of the above. Diphthongs are practised in different pitches. Then follow vowels and diphthongs in connection with consonants, next syllables and words. The pentachord is extended to the scale. The chord of three and four notes is presented in different keys.

From twenty to thirty songs are practised in addition to the religious music. Songs are sung in unison and by ear. Singing by note and in two parts can only be practised under specially favorable conditions. A secular or religious song should begin or close all school sessions In this way songs are best fixed in the memory of the pupils.

GYMNASTICS.

1. Exercises on the horizontal bar, and in standing.
2. Exercise with a stick; high jumping.
3. Exercises in drilling, and upon the parallel bars.
4. Exercises in hopping, and upon the horizontal bar.
5. Exercises in running, and upon the parallel bars.

Simple gymnastic exercises for the lowest class should be given in the pauses.

MANUAL TRAINING FOR THE GIRLS.

The end of this instruction is to fit the girls for domestic life. Industry should be encouraged, and a taste for neatness in personal appearance and economy in clothing. The following should be taught:—

(*a*) *Knitting.*—Pupils should learn to do all work of this kind required in ordinary domestic life.

(*b*) *Sewing.*—Pupils should learn the different plain stitches and patching.

(*c*) Easy work in sewing and stitching articles of clothing, etc., outlining, darning.

(*d*) More difficult work in sewing and stitching articles of clothing, the cutting of linen.

Fancy stitches should not be taught in the Elementary Schools. Practical plain sewing is the aim of the course. With this end in view the children should repair and make articles of clothing under the direction of the teachers, bringing the necessary materials from home.

It is not enough for a teacher to show how a thing is to be done. The pupils' work must be carefully controlled, and they must be taught the technical terms necessary to express intelligently what they are doing.

Local School authorities decide as to the necessity of instruction upon the sewing machine.

The teacher should keep a record of the work done by pupils.

APPENDIX G.

COURSE OF STUDY IN NORMAL SCHOOLS (PRUSSIA).

PEDAGOGICS.

Third Class (two hours weekly).

The pupils learn the most important features in the history of education through pictures of famous educators, notable periods the most interesting and useful improvements in elementary schools. This instruction is completed by the introduction of the chief pedagogical works, especially those published since the Reformation. Reading centralizes around some important pedagogical question until same be understood by pupils in all its bearings.

Second Class (two hours weekly).

General principles of education. Instruction. Form in which instruction should be given. Development through instruction. Reference is made to logic and psychology.

First Class (three hours weekly).

Methods. The teacher's position. School government. School organization.. School law. The third hour is devoted, in the practice school, to practical applications of methods learned by the pupils.

LANGUAGE.

Third Class (five hours weekly).

(*a*) Grammar: Simple, Complex and Compound sentences; parts of Speech, declensions, comparison of adjectives, conjunctions; the rules of orthography and punctuation.

(*b*) Reading: Practice in reading aloud and in written expression, form and construction of poetry, meter, rhyme; lyric and epic poetry; the poetical narrative, legend, saying, fairy tale, ballad; didactical forms, fable, parable.

Second Class (five hours weekly).

(*a*) Grammar: More difficult work in the analysis of sentences; composition of words; rules relating to verbs, adjectives and prepositions; punctuation.

(*b*) Reading, as above, with more difficult selections; lyric, epic and dramatic poetry in general; songs of the people, odes, ballads, romances, epics and dramas.

(*c*) Method in teaching reading; practical application in the form of class exercises.

First Class (two hours).

Review: Extension of the matter in reading; method in language, work in connected form, illustrated by class exercises. In language work careful attention should be paid to:

(*a*) Fluent and correct expression of thought.

(*b*) Correctness in written expression of thought, clearness in form and good arrangement. The pupil must learn to teach that which he has been taught. To insure this, ease and correctness in oral and written expression are necessary.

(*c*) Private reading: The books should embrace the masterpieces of national authors both in prose and poetry.

(*d*) Reading in class: Pieces are selected from the time of Luther to the present; form and subject matter are taken up; selections in readers in use in elementary schools are carefully studied; a number of poems are learned by heart.

In addition to the readers in use in the practice school, there are special Normal School readers.

HISTORY.

Third Class (two hours weekly).

Pictures in ancient history, especially the history of Greece (*a*) age of the heroes; (*b*) period of the law-givers; (*c*) the Persian wars to the death of Alexander the Great.

Rome (*a*) the Kings; (*b*) the Republic; (*c*) the fall of the Republic and the first century of the Empire.

Second Class (two hours weekly).

Country of the ancient Germans; wars with the Romans; the migration of tribes; period of the Carlovingians, especially the spread of Christianity and Charlemagne; history of the early German dynasties; the Crusades to the time of the Reformation.

First Class (two hours weekly).

The history of Brandenburg and Prussia up to date; relations with neighboring states and countries.

Method begins in the third class with drill in relating historical facts and events; continues in the second class with class exercises; closes in the first class with systematic work in the practice school.

Arithmetic and Algebra.

Third Class (three hours weekly).

The formation of figures; the four fundamental processes; decimals; common fractions, ratio and proportion; business arithmetic, including alligation, square and cube root.

Second Class (three hours weekly).

Proportions; positive and negative terms; equations of the first degree, powers and roots.

Class exercises are given, the subjects being taken from Elementary School courses of study. Pupils learn use of numerical frame and other apparatus for teaching primary arithmetic.

First Class (one hour).

Review to fix method; equations of the second degree, and, if possible, progressions and logarithms; drill, to insure ease and security in the solution of problems.

GEOMETRY.

Third Class (two hours weekly).

The triangle, the parallelogram and the circle; exercises in construction.

Second Class (two hours weekly).

Instruction as to the equality and similarity of plane figures and their computation; computation of contents of solids.

First Class.

Review with special reference to method in teaching.

In all classes pupils are drilled in the drawing of geometrical figures upon the blackboard.

The instruction is based upon text-books, and is given objectively. Clear instruction is given upon methods of teaching, suggestions as to continuation of course and ability to impart instruction.

NATURAL HISTORY, PHYSICS AND CHEMISTRY.

Third Class (four hours weekly).

(a) Natural History: The study of selected indigenous plants belonging to the commonest families; the system of Linné; Botanical morphology. In the Winter, Zoology two hours weekly.

(b) Physics: Magnetism, electricity and mechanics.

(c) Chemistry: The principal bases and their combinations, especially in relation to mineralogy. Two hours per week.

Second Class (four hours weekly).

Natural History: Study of the principal forms of seed and spore plants; system of classification; form, growth and diffusion. In the Winter knowledge of Zoology is extended. Structure of the human body and conditions of health. Two hours a week.

(b) Physics: Light; heat and sound.

(c) Chemistry: Extension of above. Organic Chemistry. Two hours a week.

Methods of teaching these subjects receive careful attention through lectures and class exercises.

First Class (two hours weekly).

Review and completion of the course, with special attention to methods of teaching.

Geology is introduced and suggestions given to aid in continuing the study.

Instruction is to be given objectively. Physics and Chemistry should not be taught without practical experimentation; Botany and Zoology without objects or good representatives of objects studied. Pure mechanical work in memorizing is forbidden.

GEOGRAPHY.

Third Class (two hours weekly).

The Geography of the Home Province, Prussia, Germany, and the rest of the globe, the former particularly, the latter superficially; the study of maps.

Second Class (two hours weekly).

Germany and Europe. Mathematical Geography. Method in teaching Geography through lectures and class exercises.

First Class (one hour weekly).

Continuation of methods; the use of atlas, wall-maps, globes, tellurians and other objects employed in teaching Geography. Each pupil must have a good hand atlas for use in this work. The school text-book is an abbreviated edition of the complete work.

Drawing.

Third Class (two hours a week).

Free-hand drawing. Lines and angles. Division of the same into parts. Drawing of sections of right-angled bodies and circular bodies before the eyes of pupils. Drawing of symmetrical and ornamental figures. Mechanical drawing with rule and compass. Practice in ornamental drawing. Practice in drawing upon the blackboard.

Second Class (two hours a week).

(*a*) Elements of perspective; (*b*) free-hand drawing with black chalk, bister, sepia, etc., from plaster of Paris models and from nature. This work should be arranged according to the respective talents of pupils; (*c*) practice in drawing upon the blackboard.

First Class (one hour weekly).

(*a*) Continuation of work as above, especially as regards blackboard drawing, giving attention to work in drawing demanded in teaching other subjects; (*b*) method in teaching drawing; (*c*) suggestions to aid in continuing the work beyond the Normal School course.

Instruction in drawing should enable pupils to do all work neatly required in teaching this and other subjects, such as Geometry, Geography, etc.

PENMANSHIP.

Third Class (two hours weekly).   Second Class (one hour weekly).

The object of this course is to insure:

1. Neatness, facility and correctness in all written work.
2. A definite method for use in teaching penmanship.

GYMNASTICS.

The basis of the course in gymnastics is the "New Manual for Instruction in Gymnastics." Pupils may be brought further than the book goes. They must be able to teach systematically all exercises included in said manual.

The third and second classes have two hours of practical gymnastics per week, the first class one hour. The first class has, in addition, instruction of one hour weekly upon the structure of the human body, expedients in the case of accidents, the history and purpose of physical training, apparatus used in gymnastic exercises.

Pupils of the first class, under oversight of the teacher of gymnastics, give instruction in the practice school.

The course in Music involves both vocal and instrumental Music, practice upon the piano, organ or violin. The object of the course is the training of teachers for good work in teaching Music in the Elementary Schools, not to develop special talents at the expense of the other students. Students are taught to love the old masters and to beware of introducing their own compositions in their school districts.

www.ingramcontent.com/pod-product-compliance
Lightning Source LLC
Chambersburg PA
CBHW021938240426
43669CB00047B/460